1977

ot

RTEEN DAYS

ed for each day the book is k

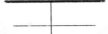

THE TASTE OF OUR TIME

Collection planned and directed by

ALBERT SKIRA

BIOGRAPHICAL AND CRITICAL STUDY

BY

TERISIO PIGNATTI

Translated from the Italian by James Emmons

CARPACCIO

SKIRA

Title page:

Scene at a Tournament, c. 1490. (17⅞×19⅜″)
Reproduced by Courtesy of the Trustees, National Gallery,
London (where it is ascribed to Domenico Morone).

★

Distributed in the United States by
THE WORLD PUBLISHING COMPANY
2231 West 110th Street, Cleveland 8, Ohio

★

© by Editions d'Art Albert Skira, 1958.
Library of Congress Catalog Card Number: 58-12919.

CARPACCIO

CARPACCIO's paintings tell us a great deal about the artist, but of the man himself and his personality we know very little. It is safe to say that he was born in Venice. He styles himself Venetian in his signatures and originally spelt his name "Scarpaza" (latinized into Carpathius, whence Carpaccio); this was a common name in Venice and the islands of the lagoon. His father was Pietro Scarpaza, a dealer in furs and hides in the parish of San Raffaele.

The year of Carpaccio's birth is unknown. He is first mentioned in the will of his uncle Fra Ilario in 1472; from this Gustav Ludwig and Pompeo Molmenti inferred that he was born about 1455, on the ground that no one under fifteen could legally be an heir. But such was not in fact the case. It was perfectly lawful to institute a child as heir; fifteen was merely the legal age for entering into possession of an inheritance. Carpaccio may well have been quite a small boy in 1472.

His name is mentioned for the second time in 1486, when he paid the rent of his father's shop, located under the arcades of the Procuratie Vecchie in the Piazza San Marco. The wording of the document suggests that he was not yet independent of his family.

When next we hear of him he is a full-fledged artist, signing and dating the *Arrival at Cologne*, first of his famous cycle of paintings illustrating the Legend of St Ursula. This was in 1490, which date may be taken as roughly indicating his début as a painter; this is borne out by the style of the work, still hesitant and immature.

A few other dates, all connected with his work, enable us to trace his career. The last painting in the St Ursula series is datable to about 1500. Having made a name for himself, he was asked to do a painting in the Sala dei Pregadi in the Ducal Palace; this canvas was destroyed in the fire of 1577. From 1502 to 1507 he worked in the Scuola degli Schiavoni, and there produced his masterpiece. The decorations in the Scuola degli Albanesi are altogether a lesser work; this is a group of six canvases, one of which bears the date 1504. In 1507 he executed two large historical paintings for the Ducal Palace: *Pope Alexander III in the Church of St Mark's* and *The Meeting of the Pope and the Doge at Ancona* (these too were destroyed in the fire of 1577). We can judge of Carpaccio's reputation by the fact that in 1508 he was called in to estimate the value of Giorgione's frescos on the outer wall of the Fondaco dei Tedeschi or German merchants' hall.

In 1511 the Marquis of Mantua was negotiating with him for a View of Jerusalem. He had already begun work on decorations in the Scuola di Santo Stefano, which he pursued at a leisurely pace until 1520. But he was getting on in years and losing something of his vigor. His style had gone out of fashion and his commissions were not so considerable as they had once been. Henceforth he worked chiefly in the outlying districts around Venice: at Treviso in 1515, at Capodistria in 1516, at Pirano and Pozzale di Cadore in 1518, at Chioggia in 1520. His last paintings, dated 1523, were again made at Capodistria. He is last mentioned alive in a document of October 28, 1525; another, dated June 26, 1526, relating to his son Pietro, refers to him as deceased.

Carpaccio was survived by his two sons, Benedetto and Pietro, indifferent painters who perpetuated their father's style until about 1550. They seem to have settled in Istria, where their descendants lived until very recently.

No self-portrait is known to exist, yet Carpaccio was famous in his day as a portrait painter. We can only suppose that if ever he portrayed his own features, he lent them, in a whimsical moment, to one of the innumerable personages who appear in his pictures. Sometimes indeed, in an ambassador or nobleman, in this or that figure who looks out from a crowd or procession, we feel we may have encountered the keen or quizzical glance of the artist himself.

Carpaccio is one of many artists who have been "resurrected" by modern criticism. If we are now in a position to appreciate the full savor of his characteristic style, this is due almost entirely to the discriminating reappraisal of the art of the past that has been (and is still being) carried out by present-day art historians.

The early historians of Italian art, from Vasari (1511-1574) to Carlo Ridolfi (c. 1598-1650), dismissed him as an undistinguished follower of Giovanni Bellini. The first clear-sighted evaluation of Carpaccio was that of Zanetti in the 18th century, who called attention to the "fanciful" nature of his creations. But the rise of Neo-Classicism made Carpaccio seem too much of a Primitive and his reputation again suffered an eclipse, although Luigi Lanzi in his study of Venetian painting (1796) emphasized his debt to Gentile Bellini rather than to Giovanni Bellini or Alvise Vivarini; the extent of this debt was elucidated by Cavalcaselle in the 19th century.

The imaginative, fanciful, "inspired" qualities of Carpaccio's art were extolled by Ruskin, certainly the most enthusiastic (if not the most illuminating) of his admirers so far. Thus we reach the modern era of art criticism. Berenson classified him as a painter of pageantry, also of familiar and homely scenes, while Lionello Venturi enlarged upon his delightful gift of storytelling and his kaleidoscopic evocations of Venice in her prime.

Gustav Ludwig and Pompeo Molmenti sifted all the known biographical and documentary material relating to the artist and the paintings, while Adolfo Venturi assessed Carpaccio's remarkable handling of color and demonstrated its functional importance in the poetic imagery of his style.

More recently Giuseppe Fiocco has investigated anew Carpaccio's debt to Antonello da Messina and the Flemish masters; Roberto Longhi has pointed out and defined the highly characteristic "spatial geometry" which links him up with Tuscan painting; and C. L. Ragghianti sees him as a creator of images whose symbolism cannot be overlooked.

Carpaccio is the last great poet of the century of Humanism, just as it was being eclipsed by the towering achievements of Cinquecento naturalism. As we shall see, an early familiarity with Ferrarese art led him to practise an architectonic representation of space which enabled him to make the most of the crystalline colors of Antonello and his followers. This synthesis, though it sometimes resulted in works that have much in common with those of the great Venetians from Bellini to Giorgione, was the product of an entirely different cultural background. While the path opened up by these men led directly to the naturalism of Titian, the poetic painting of Carpaccio diverged into a secret domain of its own where forms tended to develop into images abstract in meaning: symbols which the modern sensibility alone has understood and fully appreciated.

THE EARLY PHASE

IT is not very difficult to infer the story of Carpaccio's beginnings from the stylistic evidence of the *Christ with Four Disciples* in the Contini Collection in Florence. This is a small panel with the half-length figure of Christ in the center, lifting one hand in benediction and holding the ball of the world in the other. Grouped around him are two bearded apostles and two beardless youths. Below, on the parapet, is the artist's signature, the only one in which his name occurs in the same spelling as in the earliest records relating to him: Vetor Scarpazo. The indecision of the style makes it clear that this is a youthful work. Only a beginner could collect so many explicit mementos of well-known Venetian works of the previous decades: Antonello's *Salvator Mundi* (National Gallery, London), with the characteristic "spatial" gesture of the hand; the altarpiece recently painted by Antonello for the Venetian church of San Cassiano (now in Vienna); Giovanni Bellini's San Salvatore *Christ* (now in the Venice Academy); and several portraits by Gentile Bellini, sharply profiled against dark backgrounds. The last-named works bring us up to the years 1485-1490, and this may be taken as the most plausible date of the Contini *Christ*.

But who was this young man named Carpaccio, still groping for his way among the masters who had regenerated Venetian painting in the second half of the 15th century? All things considered, he then stood at no great distance from Antonello's leading follower at that time, Alvise Vivarini, whose pupil he may have been. His color (ultimately deriving from Mantegna) has an enamel-like brilliance and forms shifting patterns against an intricate design of incisive folds and profiles. In these years a whole group of young artists was being trained in Vivarini's workshop: Cima da Conegliano, the Venetian Marco Basaiti, and Montagna and Buonconsiglio, both natives of Vicenza.

CHRIST WITH FOUR DISCIPLES,
C. 1490. (23 ⅝ × 23 ¼″)
CONTINI COLLECTION, FLORENCE.

Each was engaged in working out a style of his own on the basis of that common artistic heritage left to them by Antonello da Messina in the masterpieces he painted at Venice during his brief visit there in 1475-1476.

Yet something in the Contini *Christ* gives us notice that this "Vetor Scarpazo" is an artist who will go a long way: it is the composition of the picture, based on an unusual architectonic structure, and this in itself is already a remarkable feature of his work. Christ is the mainstay of a firmly constructed figure group, which appears to be laid out along an inclined plane in which the heads of the four apostles mark four points on an elliptical curve rotating around the pyramidal hub of Christ's figure. The effect of this minutely calculated structure is to weld the five figures into an "architectonic unity." This, perhaps, is already an advance on the simple "geometric form" of Antonello and Alvise Vivarini; and when we remember that about the same time Giovanni Bellini was striving with all his might to create a "chromatic unity" by atmospheric gradations of tone, then we are made aware of a very definite and progressive trend—and one that was soon to be fundamental—in the painting of young Carpaccio.

There is a *Virgin and Child with Saints* at Vicenza in which, though its colors are too worn and faded to tell us much, the painter seems to tackle the same problem of pictorial architecture (and it is chiefly on this account that I am willing to accept its attribution to Carpaccio). The figures become elements of a spatial counterpoint and form a rhythmic colonnade leading up to the solemn climax of the central throne.

Perhaps the weakness of these early works is the absence of a positive feeling for color, nor was their sound structural functionalism the most suitable corrective for it. Nevertheless, the members of the Scuola (i.e. guild or confraternity) di Sant' Orsola having decided in 1488 to decorate their guild-hall,

Carpaccio must even then have been meditating those canvases which proved to be matchless miracles of color. So it is only natural to look for some transition, some intermediate stage, between his early Antonellesque experiments in crystalline form and the kaleidoscopic world of the *Legend of St Ursula*. I am inclined to ascribe his newly awakened sense of color to an experience altogether foreign to the art world of Venice, and one for which the young artist had been fully prepared by his apprenticeship in the school of Antonello: an initiation into Ferrarese art.

By the second half of the 15th century, under the Dukes of Este, Ferrara had come to rank as one of the leading art centers of Italy. Visited by Piero della Francesca and Rogier van der Weyden, Ferrara imbibed something of the aspiring spirituality of these two great exponents of the Tuscan and Flemish schools. Hence, on the one hand, the high formal abstraction and flawless geometry of Ferrarese painting and, on the other, its intense, dramatic sublimation of the real. Then came Andrea Mantegna, a more complaisant popularizer of the humanist vision which had been taking shape in Tuscany, and Ferrara now brought forth several of the major Italian artists of the time: the architect Biagio Rossetti and the painters Cosimo Tura, Francesco del Cossa and Ercole de' Roberti. Thanks to them the streets and palaces of the city gained a new splendor; in the frescos of the Palazzo Schifanoia, above all, Cossa and Roberti produced a lovely, graceful reflection of the urbane, many-sided life of Renaissance Ferrara in the form of a "court epic." At the same time a nobleman of Ferrara, Matteo Maria Boiardo, Count of Scandiano, was composing his great poem: *Orlando Innamorato*.

The lessons of Piero, Mantegna and the Flemings were taken to heart by the Ferrarese painters and reinterpreted in a style which, while varying much from artist to artist, served to express a rational-minded, humanistic vision avid of a deeper

PORTRAIT OF A MAN WITH A RED CAP, C. 1490. (13¾×9″)
MUSEO CORRER, VENICE.

life-experience and a more intense and intimate knowledge of the world. In this cultural development the function of Tuscan "perspective," a legacy of Piero, was to organize their vision of nature, while the Flemish realism bequeathed by Van der Weyden gave them the means of sharing more fully in the daily life of the community.

Here at Ferrara then we find the same forces at work which had contributed to shaping the art of Antonello da Messina, himself so much indebted to the Flemish masters and to Piero della Francesca. The circumstantial evidence all points to the likelihood that young Carpaccio, schooled in the entourage of Antonello, somehow acquired a firsthand knowledge of Ferrarese painting. It would have been an experience naturally congenial to him, and stimulated his latent gift for color.

But let us recapitulate. What grounds are there for the hypothesis that Carpaccio's training was in part Ferrarese? First and foremost, there is the internal evidence of his first masterpiece at the Scuola di Sant'Orsola, whose lucid architectonic vision and measured spatial resonance presuppose an experience that Venice could not have given him.

All the clues we have go to confirm this hypothesis. Even before evaluating the very marked Ferrarese elements embodied in the canvases that make up the *Legend of St Ursula*, we can safely ascribe to Carpaccio other works in which these elements are clearly present. The first, whose attribution is sanctioned by a large body of authoritative critics, is the *Portrait of a Man with a Red Cap* (Museo Correr, Venice). It is an exceptionally fine piece of painting and not inconsistent with later portraits by Carpaccio. The maker of this portrait undoubtedly moved in a milieu steeped in Ferrarese and Flemish influences (going from Cossa's portraits in the Palazzo Schifanoia up to Memling), yet he retained the color background which unmistakably recalls Antonello in his final phase, that of his Venetian portraits.

While this initial instance is by no means conclusive, it is certainly suggestive. And it is supported by other "Ferrarese" works, notably two *Scenes at a Tournament* (National Gallery, London, there catalogued under the name of Domenico Morone, a minor Veronese contemporary of Carpaccio) which, on the strength of their similarities with the St Ursula series, have been very plausibly attributed to Carpaccio by Roberto Longhi. The vivacity of these small figures, sketched in with quick dabs of the brush, with a light and crystalline touch, certainly points to Carpaccio. But what has hitherto passed unnoticed is the similarity to the "cavalcade" of Cossa's Schifanoia frescos at Ferrara. And the connection of these *Scenes at a Tournament* with Ferrara is materially proved in an unexpected way: above the grand stand floats a banner with the black eagle of the arms of the House of Este.

The hypothesis of Carpaccio's early contacts with Ferrara is further strengthened by the artist's relations later in life with the city of the Estes. His *Death of the Virgin* was painted in 1508 for the church of Santa Maria in Vado in Ferrara. Add to this the fact that as early as the 17th century the *Lamentation over the Dead Christ* (now in Berlin) and the *Meditation on the Passion* (Metropolitan) were owned by the Canonici family of Ferrara.

Ferrara in Carpaccio's day was a populous city where the arts and graces of life flourished under an enlightened aristocracy; a wealthy middle class carried on a thriving commerce, and the calm well-being of the place differed little from that of Venice. Carpaccio, the painter of the Venetian middle class, could not but find Ferrara to his liking. Possibly he paid the city no more than a brief visit or two and may have produced no outstanding works there. Nevertheless his contact with it was the decisive experience of his apprenticeship as a painter, and one that enabled him to express himself in the mature, unfaltering style of the *Legend of St Ursula*.

SKETCH FOR THE BACKGROUND OF THE DEPARTURE OF URSULA AND ETHERIUS,
1495. (6¾×7½″) PEN AND RED CHALK. BRITISH MUSEUM, LONDON.

THE LEGEND OF ST URSULA

LITTLE is known about the Scuola di Sant'Orsola, founded on July 15, 1300. There has been much conjecture, none of it convincing, about the location of the chapel where the Scuola had its seat. Documents record the fact that the chapel was built in 1306 in the monks' cemetery behind the apses of the church of San Zanipolo. Our scrutiny of Jacopo de' Barbari's famous topographical plan of Venice (1500) has enabled us to identify the original Scuola di Sant'Orsola almost certainly with the small building visible just to the right of the wall surrounding the apses. Access was had from the side, by passing under a small portico, and the interior was illuminated by a narrow window at the back, apparently above the altar.

In 1488 it was decided to decorate the chapel with eight canvases illustrating the story of St Ursula. The work was entrusted to Carpaccio, and the expenses were probably borne in large part by the Loredans, a patrician family whose generous patronage of the Scuola is a matter of record.

That the story, or rather legend, of St Ursula was one of the most popular subjects of late medieval art is proved by the many versions of it, in many countries. Suffice it to mention the 14th-century frescos of Tomaso da Modena at Treviso, the miniatures and woodcuts in incunabula dealing with the lives of the saints, and Memling's beautiful reliquary-shrine in the Hôpital Saint-Jean at Bruges. The story of Ursula's mission and martyrdom is told in the *Golden Legend*, a collection of saints' lives compiled by Jacobus de Voragine (c. 1230-c. 1298), archbishop of Genoa, which was one of the most widely read books of the late Middle Ages, and Carpaccio must have seen the magnificent edition of this work, translated from the Latin by Nicolò Malerbi into a vivid and ingenuous Italian and printed by Nicolas Jenson (Venice, 1475). The painter followed this text with few deviations, these no doubt being prompted by his own fancy—a young man's fancy. For it is precisely in the scenes dealing with the young prince's devoted love for Ursula that Carpaccio's imagination dilates and rises to a wonderful variety and splendor; such scenes as the Reception of the Ambassadors and the Departure of the Virgins under the leadership of Ursula, while the prince follows, faithful to the last.

The story gave full scope to Carpaccio's imagination, with its crowd scenes, its adventurous wanderings through foreign lands and towns, and the tale of Etherius and Ursula unfolds like a costumed pageant in the festival-loving Venice of the 15th century.

About 150 years after the completion of the paintings the original Scuola di Sant'Orsola was demolished and entirely rebuilt flush against the apse of the church. This event is recorded in an inscription of 1647. In the process nearly all the canvases had to be cut down to adapt them to the new wall surfaces, a strip of about ten centimeters being sheared off on two sides. In the course of time they underwent several restorations, those of the 18th and 19th centuries being particularly regrettable.

In 1810 the Scuola was suppressed and the building it had occupied was merged into a larger complex of buildings. The paintings were then transferred to the Gallerie dell'Accademia, where they may be seen today, presented exactly as they originally stood in the old Scuola di Sant'Orsola. The narrative order of the pictures does not, however, correspond to the order in which they were actually painted. The reason probably was that at the outset Carpaccio had only a limited wall space at his disposal, all the rest being taken up by the burial vaults of the Loredan family; these were removed little by little from 1492 on and the cycle of paintings could accordingly be expanded.

The first scene (in the order of the narrative) is the *Reception of the Ambassadors*. These are envoys of the king of England who

have come to seek the hand of Ursula in marriage on behalf of Conon, the English king's son. On the upper right, in her chamber, is Ursula herself, daughter of Theonotus, king of Brittany; her conditions to the marriage are that the heathen prince shall be baptized (after baptism he changes his name to Etherius, i.e. pure in soul) and allow her a respite of three years in which to make a pilgrimage to Rome with her 11,000 virgin companions. The setting is ostensibly the Court of Brittany, but the lagoon dotted with ships, the costumes of passers-by, and even the buildings (explicitly modeled on those of Mauro Coducci, the creator of Renaissance architecture in Venice) leave no doubt as to the site and scenery that really inspired the painter.

The *Dismissal of the Ambassadors*, with King Theonotus conveying Ursula's reply to the envoys, takes place in an

LEGEND OF ST URSULA: THE DISMISSAL OF THE AMBASSADORS, C. 1500.
(9 FT. 2 IN.× 8 FT. 3 IN.) GALLERIE DELL'ACCADEMIA, VENICE.

architectural setting that might be the Ducal Palace, with high
walls patterned with marble inlays of the kind made popular

by Pietro, Antonio and Tullio Lombardo. Again, in the *Return of the Ambassadors* (to the English Court), the crowd streaming over the bridge and along the quays is, as always, the motley, roistering crowd of Renaissance Venice. Here, as in all the canvases of the series, there is an extraordinary variety of rich costumes, made all the more striking by the unerring fidelity with which they are rendered: from the "Compagno della Calza" in the center of the *Reception*, with the badge of the Compagnia degli Ortolani on his shoulder, to the fashionable young men who, in spite of their vacant stare, have the personalized features of individual portraits. Then, in the *Dismissal*, there is the delightful detail of the young scribe (see p. 35)

LEGEND OF ST URSULA: THE RETURN OF THE AMBASSADORS, C. 1500. (9 FT. 8½ IN. × 17 FT. 3 IN.) GALLERIE DELL'ACCADEMIA, VENICE.

intently writing at the dictation of a gentleman who is punctuating his words with a gesture. Or various details in the *Return*, such as the lord chamberlain, the tiny rebec-player, and the monkey crouching on the steps.

The *Departure of Ursula and Etherius*, the largest painting in the series, represents two successive episodes separated by the flag-pole in the center. On the left is the English harbor, with Etherius taking leave of his father. He is about to embark for Brittany; his ship is riding at anchor, its sail bellying in the wind; but inscribed on the sail, upside down, is the word "malo," an ill omen for Etherius, auguring a voyage from which he will not return (a further portent of evil is the scorpion on the base of the flag-pole). To the right of the pole the scene changes to Brittany, the kingdom of Ursula's father. Prince Etherius has just landed and Ursula gives him welcome; as he kneels before her their eyes meet for the first time. Beneath the arc of their clasped hands is the motionless figure of an oarsman, a melancholy figure full of sad augurs, and Ursula's maid-in-waiting too turns toward us a melancholy face. On the right, the kneeling couple receive the king's embrace. In the background we see them taking ship, bound now for Rome.

We can only speculate as to the significance of the banner flying in the center, which bears the arms of a noble family of Sebenico (Šibenik) in Dalmatia. Equally mysterious is the significance of the two landscapes: on the left, a harbor entrance guarded by two lordly fortresses; on the right, a smiling prospect of palatial buildings. The two fortresses have now been identified (from the woodcuts of Erhard Reeuwich illustrating Bernhard von Breydenbach's *Opusculum Sanctarum Peregrinationum in Terram Sanctam*, published at Mainz in 1486) as those of Rhodes and Candia. The palaces are composed of a luminous variant of the Ca' d'Oro and a handsome but unidentifiable (or imaginary) Renaissance building.

LEGEND OF ST URSULA: THE DEPARTURE OF URSULA AND ETHERIUS, 1495.
(9 FT. 2 IN. × 22 FT. 4 IN.) GALLERIE DELL'ACCADEMIA, VENICE.

It may be wondered whether in Carpaccio's world, imbued with poetry yet always so transparently "real," these arbitrary insertions were made with any significant purpose in mind. It is precisely here, however, that we touch on the special character of Carpaccio's "reality": all the elements of his pictures stem from the visible world, but their pictorial relationships are an imaginative recreation transcending the limits of mere anecdote. This being so, there is no point in attaching much importance to the problem of the fortresses, whether sketched by the artist on the spot during a voyage to the Eastern Mediterranean (an old tradition, recorded in Vecellio's *Habiti*, published in Venice in 1590, affirms that Carpaccio made such a voyage) or simply copied from Reeuwich's woodcuts. The latter hypothesis is scarcely credible in view of the wealth of detail included by Carpaccio (but not by Reeuwich); still, he may have found these details in other prints available at the time.

SKETCH FOR THE DREAM OF ST URSULA, 1495? (4×4¼")
PEN AND WASH. UFFIZI, FLORENCE.

But to come back to the story of Ursula. On the way to
Rome the tidings of her martyrdom are announced to her in a
dream. The final painting of the *Dream of St Ursula* has been
cut down at the top and is not so spacious and airy as the
preliminary sketch in the Uffizi (which includes an extra window
and a broader wall on the left), but it remains, with its luminous,
spellbound calm, the most fascinating and original of Carpaccio's

works. Myrtle and pinks on the window sill symbolize love and marriage. Ruskin comments on the picture at length, with almost reverent enthusiasm, in several of the letters of *Fors Clavigera*.

LEGEND OF ST URSULA: THE DREAM OF ST URSULA, 1495? (9 FT. × 8 FT. 9 IN.) GALLERIE DELL'ACCADEMIA, VENICE.

LEGEND OF ST URSULA: THE ARRIVAL AT ROME, C. 1495.
(9 FT. 2½ IN. × 10 FT.) GALLERIE DELL'ACCADEMIA, VENICE.

In the *Arrival at Rome* Ursula, Prince Etherius, and their
retinue of virgins kneel before Pope Cyriacus, who receives
the pilgrims beneath the walls of the Castel Sant'Angelo. This
picture is unusual for its portraits, including Cardinal Domenico
Grimani (left center, in white robes), the Venetian ambassador
Niccolò Michiel (center, in red), and (presumably) Francesco

Arzentin on the right (his armorial bearings appear on several pennants). The Castel Sant'Angelo had recently been restored,

LEGEND OF ST URSULA: THE ARRIVAL AT COLOGNE, 1490.
(9 FT. 2 IN. × 8 FT. 4 IN.) GALLERIE DELL'ACCADEMIA, VENICE.

and Carpaccio may have painted it from the rather sketchy image of it on a medal struck by Pope Alexander VI in 1495 to commemorate the completed work of restoration.

Joined by Pope Cyriacus (an Englishman) and a host of bishops, Ursula turned northward again and sailed down the Rhine. The *Arrival at Cologne* shows the city being besieged by the Huns. Surprised by the barbarians, the pilgrims are massacred, one and all. In the foreground of the *Martyrdom* we see Ursula kneeling in prayer; having spurned the marriage proposal of the son of the Hunnish king, she is about to be trans-fixed by an arrow. A tall column divides the *Martyrdom* from the *Funeral* on the right, where we find the Loredan arms and several family portraits, including that of Eugenia Caotorta, wife of Angelo Loredan, who died about the time the painting was made; in accordance with an archaic iconographic tradition, Carpaccio places her outside the main scene.

So much for the story itself. We have already noted that the pictures were not painted in narrative order. As far as we can tell from the dates we have and from the study of their stylistic development, Carpaccio first painted the *Arrival at Cologne* (1490), then the *Martyrdom and Funeral* (1493), followed by the *Departure of Ursula and Etherius* (1495), the *Dream of St Ursula* (1495?), the *Arrival at Rome* (c. 1495) and last of all the *Reception, Dismissal* and *Return of the Ambassadors*. The painting of the *Legend of St Ursula* thus occupied about ten years of the artist's life, and those were decisive years for Carpaccio.

What a distance separates the three Ambassador scenes from the early *Arrival at Cologne*, reminiscent of a northern miniature, as it stretches away to a distant vanishing point beyond the floating galleons, corbelled towers and long stretch of water. The painter's undeveloped narrative gift is lavished with juvenile gusto on trivial details: banners and pennants flapping in the wind, greetings exchanged by passing soldiers beside

LEGEND OF ST URSULA: MARTYRDOM AND FUNERAL OF ST URSULA, 1493.
(8 FT. 10½ IN.× 18 FT. 4½ IN.) GALLERIE DELL'ACCADEMIA, VENICE.

the conical tents pitched under the city walls, guardsmen in the
tower excitedly pointing to the ships. Is this a scene of martial
exercise, a dramatic presage of impending death? A burnished
reflection in the water beneath the drawbridge is enough, or the
soft green moss at the water's edge clinging to the pink bricks,
and Carpaccio lets himself go, plying his brush with all the
loving attention to detail which he so much admired in the work
of the Flemish masters. With the result that dramatic effect is
sacrificed beyond recall, together with unity of perspective and
the spatial value of colors.

We get our first glimpse of the real Carpaccio in the
Martyrdom, built up in careful perspective around the descending
line of tall trees and centered on the graceful figure of a helmeted
warrior in the act of sheathing his sword. And, as if to lay
a double stress on the compositional scheme, it is precisely

LEGEND OF ST URSULA: THE DEPARTURE OF URSULA AND ETHERIUS (DETAIL),
1495. GALLERIE DELL'ACCADEMIA, VENICE.

at this point that the banner is planted, unfurled at the top of a
thin pole against a bright sky. The mature Carpaccio stands
revealed in the *Funeral of St Ursula*, in which, for the first time,

the leading figures are representative of that Venetian middle class which found in Carpaccio its most authentic poet. Here is a host of figures, easily yet strikingly posed, who stand out against a scenographic background true to the last detail, in the full flush of broad daylight which defines the plasticity of forms with amazing clarity.

The *Departure of Ursula and Etherius* perhaps best exemplifies the smooth vitality and skill with which the narrative unfolds.

LEGEND OF ST URSULA: THE RETURN OF THE AMBASSADORS (DETAIL), C. 1500. GALLERIE DELL'ACCADEMIA, VENICE.

It matters little whether the men of quality accompanying Etherius and his father are portraits of the Loredans themselves, who commissioned the paintings. The galleon that has capsized and the other with the wind in its sail, the crowd on the shore and the loiterers on the bridge and terrace, all play their part in a well-coordinated, highly animated scene, a miraculous transmutation of concrete things into the creative symbol of all the beauty and color of 15th-century Venice.

Here again, undeniably, we are reminded of the pictorial vision of the Ferrarese and Flemish masters, which Carpaccio had assimilated from the resplendent frescos in the Palazzo Schifanoia. Indeed his debt is made perfectly clear by a comparison with other scenes of procession and pageantry produced in these very years by the painters who were decorating the Ducal Palace and the Scuola di San Giovanni Evangelista: Gentile Bellini, Lazzaro Bastiani and Giovanni Mansueti. There is a three-dimensional vitality in Carpaccio's figures that is quite lacking in Gentile's nerveless puppets (not to mention those of Bastiani and Mansueti), reduced as they are to wooden profiles against a backdrop of stage-sets devoid of spatial recession, in the muddled focus of a perspective that can only be described as medieval.

In the *Departure*, on the contrary, the eye sees deep into space, sweeps freely across the measured expanse of sea and shore, and is met by detail after detail accurately rendered and brought vividly to life: the footbridge whose broad planks are fitted together with the precision of a skilled carpenter, the Turkey carpets in the center foreground, the cluster of oars around the small boat which is about to carry the young couple out to their waiting ship in the roadstead. Every component of the intricate network of spatial relationships set up by these objects has a vitality of its own, owing to the light that plays upon them.

LEGEND OF ST URSULA: THE DISMISSAL OF THE AMBASSADORS (DETAIL),
C. 1500. GALLERIE DELL'ACCADEMIA, VENICE.

LEGEND OF ST URSULA: THE RETURN OF THE AMBASSADORS (DETAIL),
C. 1500. GALLERIE DELL'ACCADEMIA, VENICE.

Similar influences went to shape Carpaccio's conception of
color, which he handled in a manner altogether alien to the
Venetian tradition, a manner indebted rather to the color-light
synthesis of the Tuscans and the Northerners. Diverging now

36

from the crystalline clarity and fully modeled plasticity of Antonello da Messina and his followers, Carpaccio's color in the *Departure* is graduated into local values enhanced by a steady play of vibrant light. All the figures standing on the footbridge in the foreground are like many-faceted prisms drinking in the light, which washes over them profusely and throws this or that patch of color into brilliant relief. Here is a new style or idiom of color-light on the rise in Venice, alongside—and in opposition to—that of Giovanni Bellini. It is a style anything but sensual, devoid of musicality in the purely lyrical sense, and devoid too of the softly blended tones of Italian *sfumato*; it is above all clean-cut, measured, well-proportioned.

These qualities were the fruit of an evolutionary process which may be traced by comparing the crowd in the *Departure* with that, slightly later in date, in the *Return of the Ambassadors*. In both the glancing light indicates planes with great precision; but in the latter the almost incredible "bouquet" of red, green, blue and yellow hats seems to absorb the painter's entire attention, and he turns it into a flower-show of delicately resonant colors above the heads of these Venetian notables.

Yet (and this is the fundamental principle of his poetic style) Carpaccio never sacrifices accurate spatial representation to color effects. On the contrary, as pictures come from his brush, their spatial and atmospheric unity is progressively deepened and consolidated as he becomes adept, amazingly adept, at rendering perspective. As time goes on, the great towers in the *Departure*, which fail to rise above the decorative effect of marquetry (an effect accentuated by the precision and finish of the drawing), are transformed into the fabulous dream-city of the *Return of the Ambassadors*. Reflected in limpid waters, it seems to be fashioned, house by house, stone by stone, by a piercing light which engraves their flawless lines and sublimates them to a symbol of repose and certitude and solemnity.

In this light-filled world Carpaccio concentrates his poetry on particular details which, by virtue of the formal perfection to which he develops them, become consummate images in their own right, symbols of a figurative abstraction in which every object might be detached from the whole and stand by itself in the magic light of poetry. Perhaps the first example that comes to mind is the famous Scribe in the *Dismissal of the Ambassadors*, seated slightly in shadow, intent on his writing tablet. It is certainly not for the mere charm of his attitude, or for his "pretty face," that we remember him. It is because he is the pivot figure of a composition whose every detail is unforgettable: the chandelier with its pendants glittering in the varied incidence of light; the thin bright lines of the windows; the limpid prismatic pattern of the broad steps, which the pantograph unexpectedly formed by the legs of the kneeling ambassador seems to measure and define.

It is in the *Reception of the Ambassadors*, however, that we have the most astonishing examples of Carpaccio's wonderful capacity for sharpness of definition, which enables him to embrace the "real" to the exclusion of mere "realism," and to attain that plane of abstraction which might be described as a plane of poetic "indifference." Note on the left the receding arches of the portico, with its marble moldings curving in the light, of which we divine every detail, every architectural rhythm. Note the railing, whose cast shadow is like a hundred dial-hands which mark the stealing hours on the marble pavement of the royal pavilion. Note the gate opened toward us in the foreground, and sharply foreshortened with such precision that its measurements might be worked out mathematically. It seems as if it would cost no effort at all to reach out and close that gate, so easily must it swing on its oiled hinges, so precisely is it filed and grooved to fit the molded base of the marble pillar. All these things are designed with consummate technical skill

LEGEND OF ST URSULA: THE DEPARTURE OF URSULA AND ETHERIUS (DETAIL),
1495. GALLERIE DELL'ACCADEMIA, VENICE.

LEGEND OF ST URSULA: THE DEPARTURE OF URSULA AND ETHERIUS (DETAIL),
1495. GALLERIE DELL'ACCADEMIA, VENICE.

and faultless accuracy; this painting is all the blueprint a
competent workman would need to construct such a gate,
such railings, and so on.

LEGEND OF ST URSULA: THE DEPARTURE OF URSULA AND ETHERIUS (DETAIL),
1495. GALLERIE DELL'ACCADEMIA, VENICE.

Carpaccio certainly possessed the gifts that go to make a
master-builder. Compared with his, the architectural backgrounds of Gentile Bellini look like pasteboard stage-sets.

LEGEND OF ST URSULA: THE ARRIVAL AT COLOGNE (DETAIL), 1490.
GALLERIE DELL'ACCADEMIA, VENICE.

LEGEND OF ST URSULA: THE ARRIVAL AT COLOGNE (DETAIL), 1490.
GALLERIE DELL'ACCADEMIA, VENICE.

43

Carpaccio's buildings are designed with a thoughtful precision and an easy mastery of technical principles worthy in every way of a professional architect. How is it, one wonders, that the Venetians of his day failed to take the hint and embellish their city with just such a domed temple, so beautifully proportioned a creation, as we see in the *Reception of the Ambassadors*. More than a century had to elapse before Baldassare Longhena took up the idea when he came to build the church of Santa Maria della Salute. As for the luminous edifice in the *Return of the Ambassadors*, built over a broad archway and enhanced with two-light windows and marble reliefs on the façade, was it not conceived at about the same time as (possibly even before) the Palazzo Vendramin Calergi (built by Mauro Coducci), the Scuola di San Marco and the Chiesa dei Miracoli (built by Pietro Lombardo)? Perhaps some day it will be discovered that the idea for one or two of the many authorless palaces of Quattrocento Venice originated with Carpaccio, in friendly rivalry with the architects of the day.

At any event, Carpaccio was more alive than any painter in Venice to the new architecture that was then changing the face of the city. Arising in the 14th century and developing apace in the 15th, the new style of building made the most of those ogival forms which are traditionally known as Gothic, but which in this context it would be better to call "Decorated Venetian" in view of its tasteful abundance of elegant ornamentation, here dainty as lacework, there unreal and picturesque as a painting. The transition from the old Venice of red brickwork to the new Venice of white marble thus found in Carpaccio its commemorative poet, if not one of its direct initiators. For we have much more than mere copies in the many buildings and architectural details which he painted, from the different palaces discussed above to the steps leading up to thrones that occur in several pictures; from the plain, regular cornice of the pavilion in the *Return of the Ambassadors* to the double window in the *Dream of St Ursula* and the marble inlays and large doorway in the *Dismissal of the Ambassadors*. How easy it is to imagine Mauro Coducci, Pietro Lombardo, Buora, and the other great architects who worked at the Scuola di San Marco, laying down their ruler and compass of an afternoon and taking the few steps that brought them up behind the apse of San Zanipolo, beside the old Scuola di Sant'Orsola, where they watched a young painter named Scarpaza at work on his flawlessly limpid architectural creations, brushing in mullioned windows and marble inlaid façades designed after their own hearts. I, for my part, have always noticed that the best architects make a point of familiarizing themselves with the work of their painter friends; so it is today, so it may have been in Venice in the last decade of the 15th century.

Still, it must not be thought that Carpaccio was an architect who had missed his vocation; he was, first and foremost, a painter. His architectural gifts, so unusual for his day (indeed unique in contemporary Venetian painting), were stimulated by his youthful contacts with Tuscan art and culture, in which architectonic motifs were vital components of an ideal geometry whose symmetry and equilibrium greatly contributed to the spiritual foundations of Renaissance culture, and to the spiritual make-up of the men who embodied it.

Nor should it be forgotten that, in Carpaccio's case, this was an architecture of a very special kind, conceived wholly in terms of spatial conditions peculiar to Venice. It was, in a word, an architecture of polished surfaces, of glistening reflections in the water, and it drew its expressive values from the atmosphere of color that surrounded and conditioned it. So it was that in the last three canvases of the St Ursula series, painted about 1500, Carpaccio's style came to incline more and more to a studied synthesis of perspective and color.

From the early handling of color, in deft strokes of the brush enlivened by shafts of glancing light, to the broad landscape backgrounds of the three Ambassador scenes, there gradually arose a unity of atmosphere which may be described as the happy effect of a particular color tonality. In the *Reception* it is the pink of early morning in which, visible through the arcade, a gondola is crossing the lagoon toward a distant church; or the silvery grey and emerald green where the low Venetian "caorlina," all sails set, passes in the center background. In the *Return* it is the amber-colored reflection of the southern sky between the harbor towers; the limpid green of the walled garden beyond the royal pavilion and the gathered crowd on the right; or the gilded silence and all but imperceptible shadings of atmosphere in the *Dream of St Ursula*.

At first he cannot be said to have attained that complete fusion, that harmony which results when all space is resolved into color. There linger in the foreground isolated patches of vivid brushwork which sheds added luster on the silk and damask of costumes, on the red wool of a cap or the woven fabric of fine hose. But in the last pictures of the series we become aware of what, in time, was to constitute Carpaccio's major achievement in the realm of color: a mellow unity of atmosphere and a smooth gradation of tones, within the well-defined bounds of accurate perspective and the lyrical flow of poetic narrative.

Carpaccio's youthful masterpiece thus ended on a note of promise—a promise which came as the natural issue of the limpid diction of his early style. But the *Legend of St Ursula* remains an unforgettable performance in Carpaccio's best poetic vein. It is the work to which we always return when we long for a vision of the Golden Age of Venice, with her heavy-laden ships and well-filled warehouses, her cheerful inhabitants always ready to don their finest clothes and join a procession—scenes that are like an illuminated page from an old book of pageantry.

TOWARD MATURITY

THE two touchstones of Carpaccio's art are the paintings in the Scuola di Sant'Orsola and those in the Scuola degli Schiavoni. The first cycle gave the young artist an opportunity of showing what he could do, and enables us to follow the early development of his style. The second, executed between 1502 and 1507, exemplifies the style of his maturity.

No great distance separates these two sets of works. Indeed it is reasonable to suppose that the three Ambassador scenes were more or less contemporary with his preliminary studies for the initial paintings at the Scuola degli Schiavoni. At this point, however, in the closing years of the 15th century, allowance must be made for a special factor which necessarily intervened in the evolution of Carpaccio's art and whose effects need to be evaluated: the influence of the Bellinis.

Little has been said of the Bellinis in the preceding pages. Enough, however, has been said about Carpaccio himself and the formation of his style for it to be clear that no critical value can be attached to the accounts of Carpaccio handed down by Vasari and other early biographers, who all describe him as a "pupil" of Giovanni Bellini, probably on account of their common participation in the historical paintings in the Ducal Palace. It is rather with Gentile Bellini, Giovanni's elder brother, that we can establish a precise relationship. Carpaccio's senior by nearly two generations, Gentile was perhaps the most respected master in Venice at the close of the 15th century. Accredited portrait painter of the Doges, official illustrator of Venetian history, curator of the picture collections in the Ducal Palace, and head of a flourishing *bottega*, he was also the happy beneficiary of a government pension.

Gentile's paintings in the Ducal Palace perished in the great fire of 1577, but luckily we still have the *Legend of the True Cross* which he executed for the Scuola di San Giovanni Evangelista (now in the Venice Academy). This consists of the famous *Procession on Piazza San Marco* and the *Miracle-working Relic of the True Cross retrieved from the San Lorenzo Canal*, and in these we find Gentile at his best. His is a late medieval Venice, solemnly crystallized in stiff perspective, with serried processions of nobles and commoners winding across a silent, imaginary stage, in the finely chiseled immobility of a world cut off from the life-giving air and passing time of reality. His buildings, by their very immobility and rarefied precision, seem to proclaim their painted estate and essential unreality. The waters of the canal, full of monks miraculously healed by the relic of the Cross, and the sky fretted with towers and chimneys seem as solid and dense as precious minerals.

As it happened, one painting in this series illustrating the *Legend of the True Cross* was assigned to Carpaccio. His contribution was the *Healing of the Demoniac*—a miracle supposed to have occurred in the house of the Patriarch of Grado beside the Rialto Bridge. The subject differed little from that treated by Gentile Bellini in the *Relic retrieved from the San Lorenzo Canal*: a crowd on the canal banks, with the gondolas, houses, chimneys and roof-gardens (with laundry drying in the sun) so typical of old Venice. Yet these two paintings portray different worlds. Gentile's forms are governed by a cramped and arbitrary perspective and made to subserve the "official" ceremonial of the scene; Carpaccio's are organized within a sound spatial structure. Below the covered terrace on the left where the miracle is taking place, the canal bank (the old Riva del Ferro, today Riva del Vin) with its idlers and strollers recedes into the picture along an exactly measurable distance. Every foot of space is *scanned*, is fitted smoothly into a rhythmic structure marked at appropriate intervals by the foreshortened profile of a door or window, by two merchants on the canal bank sitting

LEGEND OF THE TRUE CROSS: THE HEALING OF THE DEMONIAC, C. 1495.
(12 FT. × 12 FT. 9 IN.) GALLERIE DELL'ACCADEMIA, VENICE.

over their contracts, by two bearded Turks behind them in white turbans sauntering down the steps of the Rialto Bridge.

But it is Carpaccio's light, altogether lacking in Gentile's work, that constitutes the soul of this singular painting, light that is both an instrument of knowledge and a medium of both poetic and rational experience. In this radiance Carpaccio's colors take on the localized but extremely acute vibrations of precious matter: in the costumes of gondoliers and gentlemen, in the remote details of small craft passing under the bridge, in the approaching group of gondolas coming up to a short flight of stone steps composed of innumerable facets of intersecting prisms, each of which reflects light on one plane and absorbs it on another. And here again we meet with a favorite device of Carpaccio: the amazing *trompe-l'œil* of the wooden piers supporting the bridge, which the light sharply defines and holds in focus, four-square and true—a flawless piece of construction.

Painted in the same spirit of imaginative precision, the procession appears in the middle of the drawbridge, luminous against the dark houses. Old Venetian chimneys are dotted about the roof-tops like fantastic candalabra, while the water in contrast flows darkly below and absorbs the residue of light, bringing out in sharp relief the host of tiny figures scattered over the canvas with the easy skill of a master weaver of oriental carpets. Here, certainly, are reminiscences of the *Reception* and *Return of the Ambassadors*. But a new departure has unquestionably been made: a new unity of color and atmosphere, opening up fresh possibilities of graduating color values in a picture space no longer organized simply in terms of perspective, but harmonized in accordance with the surrounding atmosphere. This development, it is safe to say, denotes the influence of Gentile's brother, Giovanni Bellini.

Whatever the extent to which Carpaccio's early training followed independent, almost un-Venetian lines, running its course between Antonello da Messina, the Flemish masters, and Ferrarese art, the fact is that no one working in late 15th-century Venice could remain unaffected by Giovanni Bellini. Virtually every artist who plied a brush in Venice or in Venetia owed him something, all had tasted of the fruit of his experience.

FRAGMENT OF A CRUCIFIXION, C. 1495. (26¾ × 16½")
UFFIZI, FLORENCE.

He himself, moreover, had never ceased to experiment with his medium and renew his style—through a continuous evolution of forms that gathered force with the years.

Giovanni Bellini's influence had a very definite and easily definable impact on Carpaccio's art. That influence bore first of all on subject matter; it affected Carpaccio's use of traditional religious iconography, but not the wayward flights of his imagination. It also led to a more delicate shading of color, and color as applied to figures no longer sublimely "indifferent," like those in the *Legend of St Ursula* and the *Healing of the Demoniac*, but to figures that are made to express thoroughly human emotions.

As to concrete examples, mention may be made of the *Christ* at Udine (1496), which even in its decorative patterns recalls Bellini's *Virgin and Child with Saints* in San Pietro Martire at Murano; the *Pietà* in the Serristori Collection in Florence, inspired by Bellini's *Pietàs* in London and Berlin (1475-1480); the *Polyptych of St Martin* in the cathedral of Zara (now Zadar, in Dalmatia), in which the landscape backgrounds tend to reabsorb the over-linear figures in the foreground. There is also the Frankfort *Virgin and Child*, which attempts an emotional harmonization difficult to attain outside the architecture of the composition, and remains too obviously Antonellesque in its crystalline fragmentation of the plastic design, built up in glassy zones of color blocked out as in the *Legend of St Ursula*. And lastly there is the very fine *Meditation on the Passion of Christ* in the Metropolitan, which must be roughly contemporary with Giovanni Bellini's *Pietà* in Stockholm (c. 1500).

The *Meditation*, very "archaic" for its period, makes it clear once more that Carpaccio had deliberately chosen to ignore the developments of Venetian painting in the past few decades. What precedents does this work bring to mind, if not certain macabre fantasies of Ercole de' Roberti such as the Berlin

THE MEDITATION ON THE PASSION, C. 1500. (27¾×38⅛")
COURTESY OF THE METROPOLITAN MUSEUM OF ART, NEW YORK.

St John, or the glossy surfaces of Cossa's Griffoni Altarpiece? These were the painter's immediate sources and most evident sympathies. Even as late as about 1500 the lessons of Ferrara were still sufficiently operative in Carpaccio's mind to suggest this shattered, richly decorated throne, these saints with skin of burnished leather, this rock-bound landscape with its bare, contorted tree—so many reminiscences of Mantegna transmitted by way of Ferrara.

Areas of color are scrupulously made to coincide with the linear design, incised with the burin and visible beneath a light glaze, and the colors themselves change with the shifting incidence and transparency of the light. Carpaccio has taken the measure of each pebble, treated as an objective spherical entity, and of every stone and boulder, treated as light-focusing prisms while casting shadows that are increasingly sharp and naturalistic—like those on a sun dial which, for Carpaccio, had failed to register the passage of time across the first great creative phase of Venetian painting, from Giovanni Bellini to Giorgione.

THE SCUOLA DEGLI SCHIAVONI

THE "Scuola Dalmata dei Santi Giorgio e Trifone," commonly called the "Scuola degli Schiavoni," is one of the few religious and charitable confraternities, so typical of old Venice, that have survived to the present day. There was a time when several dozen of these pious foundations flourished there, grouping by nationality the different religious creeds and the different craftsmen's guilds. Today there remain but five of them, most of which have long since been shorn of their art treasures. The great exception is the Schiavoni; in this respect it is one of the most precious vestiges of the Venetian past.

The Scuola degli Schiavoni (i.e. guild of the Slavonians) was founded on May 19, 1451, by the large Dalmatian colony of Venice as a place of assembly, fellowship and mutual benefit. At first it had no seat of its own, its members meeting in the Hospice of the Knights of Malta. Shortly afterwards they were granted a special altar for their private use in the church of the same Knights. Meanwhile the Scuola grew and prospered, as is proved by its relations with Cardinal Bessarion, the famous scholar. About 1480 work was finally begun on a building in which to house the Scuola, and in 1501 it was completed. Jacopo de' Barbari's old woodcut of Venice shows the building as it then was: a modest construction of about 32 by 26 feet beside the church of the Knights of Malta, with a brick façade turned slightly toward the Fondamenta (i.e. canal bank) di Sant'Antonin.

Carpaccio's paintings, on which he worked from 1502 to 1507, were hung on the walls of the upper room, framed by pilasters on either side, a simple frieze above, and a wooden socle below rising more than six feet from the floor. In 1551 the Scuola was rebuilt, but the original layout, consisting of two superimposed rooms and a sacristy, remained unchanged.

The paintings themselves, however, together with the frieze, socle and pilasters framing them, were transferred to the ground floor, where they may still be seen today.

These decorations consist of nine canvases. Except for two, of which more will be said in a moment, they illustrate the lives of the three patron saints of Dalmatia: a young knight (St George), a boy (St Tryphonius), a sage (St Jerome). Again the subject matter is taken from the *Golden Legend*, but the more modest proportions of the work, the tone of the narrative, more involved and naïve, and the new intensity of expression make for a noticeable difference of style between this work and the *Legend of St Ursula*.

No records relating to the Schiavoni decorations have yet come to light, in spite of all the researches carried out in the registers of the Scuola and the municipal archives of Venice. The dates on the paintings will have to suffice; their style in any case retains the limpidity of his previous work and evolves on lines that present no problems of critical interpretation.

The *Vocation of St Matthew*, dated 1502, reverts to the roseate colors of the *Reception of the Ambassadors*. Its setting is such as might have been observed daily in Venice. The money-changer steps from his booth in answer to the call of an exceptional visitor: the Lord. The background is painted from the life; it represents an old gateway of Venice, the Porta del Ghetto, just as it looked at that time. The *Prayer in the Garden* stands distinctly apart from the other paintings in the cycle. Stylistically, it has more in common with the Bellinesque series of slightly earlier works, and is best coupled, anyhow as far as the figures are concerned, with the Zara Polyptych.

Neither the *Vocation of St Matthew* nor the *Prayer in the Garden* forms part of the legend of the three Dalmatian saints; both, moreover, include an unidentified coat of arms, which seems to indicate that they were donated together to the Scuola by the owner of those arms. It can only be supposed (and the dimensions of the two canvases make this plausible) that they took the place of other paintings which were planned as pendants of the rest of the cycle but which for unknown reasons Carpaccio never executed. The discrepancy both of style and subject makes this a virtual certainty, and indeed it is not for these two works that the Scuola degli Schiavoni has become famous.

The cycle properly begins then with three canvases devoted to St Jerome. The first is *St Jerome in his Study*. Light pouring in obliquely through open windows illuminates a spacious room, sparsely but richly furnished, a kind of private oratory in the purest Quattrocento style, containing an altar and a book cabinet at the back, two shelves laden with books and statuettes on the left wall, and beside it a curule chair and a *prie-dieu*. In the foreground is the saint at work on his translation of the Bible. His desk—a mere plank—is covered with green cloth, fastened with golden bosses, and cluttered with books and objects: a pair of scissors, a cockle-shell, a small bell, an inkwell, and astronomical instruments including a spherical astrolabe. Making notes from three books open in front of him, Jerome pauses momentarily, casting about for the right turn of phrase. He is the very image, valid for all ages, of the scholar absorbed in his researches. He is also the symbol of Renaissance Humanism, which by now was thoroughly acclimatized in Venice, thanks to her commentators of Neo-Platonic philosophy, her translators of the Greek classics, her celebrated printers, her young intellectuals who attended the University of Padua, and her patrician collectors of antiquities and "modern" paintings, Flemish, Tuscan and also Venetian.

It has been suggested that this may be a portrait of Cardinal Bessarion, patron of the Scuola from its beginnings. It is an attractive suggestion and perfectly plausible. At one with the humanist spirit of his time, Carpaccio would no doubt have

ST JEROME IN HIS STUDY, C. 1502. (56¼ × 85½″)
SCUOLA DEGLI SCHIAVONI, VENICE.

welcomed the opportunity of thus immortalizing the man who did more than any other to introduce Greek culture into Renaissance Italy.

A word should be said about the iconographic originality of the picture. It is unique in Venetian painting for its wealth of detail, and for the painstaking analysis of objects which thus delineated, one by one, become visual symbols, pure and perfect forms. There is a rare feast for the eyes in this inexhaustible collection of curious objects whose shapes and secrets are only to be discovered little by little, over a period of time. Count the volumes on the slanting shelf on the left wall and they will be found to number exactly forty, some of them bound in red and green morocco, some in brown leather, some in ivory-colored vellum. In the cabinet at the back three books are standing open on the lectern, and a desire comes over us to turn it around and see if perhaps there is not a fourth hidden behind.

No detail has been overlooked. The door of the cabinet is fitted with its bolt; the red and green antiphonaries leaning against the wall cast their shadows, so does the Maltese puppy in the middle of the floor, the only living being besides the saint himself in this almost aquatic silence. The little animal sits motionless, his fluffy coat almost incandescent in the dazzling light; he seems to be gazing up at the fine cloud of dust particles floating down the shaft of light as it pours in from the window.

So compellingly real are these objects, so warm and tangible is their friendly presence, that unconsciously we acquire the conviction of the actual existence of that table at which the saint is seated, of the curule chair and its red leather upholstery. It has even proved possible to transcribe (as Ludwig and Molmenti showed some fifty years ago) and perform the musical scores visible beneath the table in the right foreground: one a grave and austere song for two tenors and bass, the other light and melodious, for soprano, contralto, bass and tenor.

There is no end to the scrutiny of such a picture, for obviously the artist set out to accumulate objects *ad infinitum*, a maze of "images" through which he leads the eye unfalteringly. It was a type of painting in which no one in Venice could vie with him, and which the intellectuals of the city, among them a rising young artist named Giorgione, may well have reprehended as "northern" or "Flemish." Even today, when we seek a precedent, we have no alternative but to go back to certain early Van Eycks, which Carpaccio may have seen in the great

private collections of Venice, or at the Estense Court in Ferrara. While making allowance for great stylistic differences, one cannot help thinking of certain details in Van Eyck's *Portrait of Giovanni Arnolfini and his Wife* (National Gallery, London); and of certain interiors by Van der Weyden, notably that of the Munich *Annunciation*, with its full-blooded flavor of reality (though admittedly Carpaccio's world has little else in common with this powerful evocation of supremely abstract images).

ST JEROME IN HIS STUDY (DETAIL), C. 1502.
SCUOLA DEGLI SCHIAVONI, VENICE.

The next picture in the series is *St Jerome and the Lion*. The story is that one day a wounded lion wandered into the precincts of the monastery; all the monks fled in terror except Jerome, who extracted the thorn from its paw and tended it till the wound had healed, whereupon the grateful lion became his inseparable companion. This is one of Carpaccio's most soundly constructed works, and he seems to have intended it as a kind of memorial to the Scuola where he lived and worked for five years, while producing this picture cycle. Recognizable in the background is the Scuola itself, its pink brick façade rising above an open portico; comparison with Jacopo de' Barbari's contemporary woodcut shows how very accurately Carpaccio transcribed the building, overlooking no detail of the architecture yet always rendering it as a unified whole, solid and convincing. Extending to the right behind the Scuola is the Hospice of Santa Caterina, built of the same brick. In the middle distance on the right, with its wooden entrance porch,

THE DEATH OF ST JEROME, 1502. (56¼×83¼")
SCUOLA DEGLI SCHIAVONI, VENICE.

is the church of the Knights of Malta, San Giovanni del Tempio; its exterior frescos are clearly visible on the side walls of the nave.

There is a general panic at the sight of the lion. A peacock is about to take flight, a deer is bounding across the lawn, the monks are bolting. One in his haste has thrown aside his breviary. We can almost hear the tinkling of the keys at the guardian's side as he and his fellows run for their lives, radiating in several directions around the point marked by St Jerome's staff. Two monks can be seen in the background as they make for the door of the Hospice, leaping up the steps two by two.

If the scene of *St Jerome in his Study* showed Carpaccio in a mood of happy contemplation, lingering over a great variety of still-life details, here we find him at his liveliest, organizing the successive episodes of a brisk scene of action out-of-doors in a well-defined space. The sharp lines of the narrative are vividly expressed for their own sake and they emerge with an evocative power unparalleled in his earlier work, least of all in the *Legend of St Ursula*, where they were almost always sacrificed to the scenic effect of a strictly frontal presentation in accurate perspective. Now in full possession of his means, Carpaccio went beyond the static figure arrangements of his youth, unfolding his story in the fluent rhythms of a narrative punctuated with whimsical sallies and expectant pauses.

The setting of the scene is distinctly oriental, with loitering groups of Turks, umbrella palms, and a regular zoo of exotic animals (parrots, guinea-fowl, deer, fawns, rabbits, martens, etc.). A make-believe Orient perhaps, composed of random borrowings. But the painter makes no extravagant claim on our credibility and proffers it with a smile. No more objection can be made to these things than to the Scuola and the Hospice and the Church of San Giovanni, all "borrowed" from reality, down to the last detail of doors and windows. It is idle to carp at these borrowings, they must be accepted in the spirit in which they were intended. What matters here is the story to be told, and they contribute essentially to the simplicity, liveliness and verisimilitude of it.

Again in the third and last canvas, the *Death of St Jerome*, the setting is oriental. The procession chanting the office of the dead has come to a halt under a portico, which apparently connects the monastery with the church. The saint's body is laid out on the bare stones, with a large stone serving as a pillow for his head. An old monk bent with age reads from a large Bible, while another in a purple cope gives the response; neither has forgotten his spectacles. There is the merest hint of a humorous touch in the rendering of the monks' noses, which play so prominent a part in their profiles (and this is borne out by the spirited preliminary drawings now in the Uffizi). A further note of facetious bravura is struck by the lizard in the foreground providing the sole support for the card on which the painter has signed and dated his picture; or again by the skull on the left, whose missing jawbone is to be seen just below on the edge of a holy-water basin.

The background stretches away with unusual breadth between a series of buildings grouped in perspective around the center of the courtyard, which is marked by a tall palm-tree to which a hyena is tied. Beyond the palm is a well, toward which a mounted oriental rides; to the right is St Jerome's pet lion, crouching on the warm sand and emitting a lazy roar. There is no excluding the possibility that here Carpaccio recorded his memories of some Venetian trading post in the Levant, which he may have visited in the course of a (hypothetical) voyage to the East. Nevertheless, though the "properties" in the scene are real enough in themselves to be convincing, the "climate" of the picture is not that of firsthand experience but of fable; with its ingenuous profusion of solemn and fanciful notes, this is a world of make-believe.

ST JEROME AND THE LION (DETAIL), C. 1502.
SCUOLA DEGLI SCHIAVONI, VENICE.

66

ST JEROME AND THE LION (DETAIL), C. 1502.
SCUOLA DEGLI SCHIAVONI, VENICE.

A sunny calm floats like a haze over the scene, broken only by the murmur of prayers. Even the colors are applied in broad zones conducive to a feeling of repose: the blue of the sky, the golden sands, the ivory-colored walls of old houses. The whole picture breathes peace, composure, concord, and these are the qualities with which the very style of the painting is imbued; the reason for this lies in the coherent fusion, so long sought and here achieved at last, between color as a means of expression and form as a means of spatial construction.

Analysis will show, in fact, that the *Death of St Jerome* is composed of the skillful interweaving of two lines of melody harmonically combined. In the foreground the blue and white of the monks' robes form a lively staccato which rises to a polyphonic density in the austere white of St Jerome's body, laid out against the faint pink of the stone walk. In the background the melody of the colors is low-pitched and diffuse; tones tend to mingle, and the general effect is one of grave appeasement, untroubled by loud sonorities. The spell cast by the picture is born of that contrast, or counterpoise, which leaves the mind suspended between two worlds—that of men and that of created things—in a mood of lucid contemplation, happy in the rewarded effort to gain knowledge and judge it critically; this is the spiritual secret of Carpaccio's humanism. These two melodies, these two worlds, are fused in a final synthesis of color and perspective, of reality and imagination.

We can to some extent retrace the lucid, deliberate process of creation that engendered the poetry of such a picture by taking a ruler and plotting the points of reference on which the perspective is built up: the cornices and bases of houses, the conical silhouettes of palm-trees in strictly descending perspective, the linear pattern of the flag-stones in the foreground, even the converging lines of sight of the monks. It comes as no surprise to discover that the artist planned his

THE DEATH OF ST JEROME (DETAIL), 1502.
SCUOLA DEGLI SCHIAVONI, VENICE.

picture on rigorously geometric lines, taking as the vanishing point the base of the smallest palm, in the exact center. Here is the point of focus of every element of perspective in the picture, whose constructive principles exactly correspond to those of a peep-show.

It is worth pausing for a moment at this "spatial center" of the picture, which contains *in nuce* the creative potential of all his pictures. It is the hub of a complex of "mechanisms" which interlock with the precision of clockwork: the houses with wooden balconies in front of the small portico with two arches; and, just beyond, the surrounding wall; then, just to

69

the right at the back of the picture, the gateway to the courtyard, its two swinging doors ajar. In front of this is the well, its rough-hewn pump-arm upheld by a forked treetrunk, while the lip of the well consists of four logs set in a square—a final indulgence in geometric forms for their own sake.

But this is not all. A final surprise awaits us when we realize that, underlying the primary system of perspective whose vanishing point is the distant palm-tree in the center, there is a second pattern of forms: the semicircle of monks in the fore-ground. And these forms too we find to be geometrically linked, by the invisible projection of each monk's gaze, to the body of the saint, the geometric center of which lies immediately below the main vanishing point. This secondary system of perspective, with its tighter linkage of denser forms, seems to be introduced as a counterbalance to the other; the upper vanishing point recedes from us, while the lower one is projected toward us. The result is an astonishing effect of depth and elasticity, which adds to the vivacity and tension of the narrative.

Here we have an essential feature of Carpaccio's style, one that is particularly in evidence in the Schiavoni paintings and signalizes his maturity. It is actively present in *St Jerome in his Study*. The vanishing point, thrown off-center to the right, is located directly behind the figure of the saint, at a point which coincides with his upraised hand as he pauses to gather his thoughts and choose his words. It is almost as if by his gesture —that of the conductor calling the orchestra to attention— St Jerome himself were arresting our gaze at the point most essential to the picture. So here again the geometrical patterning of forms deliberately "points" the narrative, whose deeper harmony resides in the spatial distribution of the colors.

This way of seeing, peculiar to Carpaccio, which supplies a firm structural framework for the free handling of color, also characterizes the next two paintings at the Scuola degli

Schiavoni: *St George and the Dragon* and the *Triumph of St George*. Here he dealt with a theme of romantic gallantry much in the spirit of the *Legend of St Ursula*, but approached it with far greater powers at his command. It would be hard to find, in the painting of any period, a finer St George than this blond knight on a dark steed, bearing down intrepidly on the slimy monster whose pestilential breath polluted the air, and who could only be appeased by the daily sacrifice of two youths or maidens from the neighboring town of Selene. But in St George the dragon finally met his match, and in the second picture, subdued and cringing at the feet of the victor, it is about to be slain before a large, colorful crowd, including the grateful king and his lovely daughter, Princess Sabra, whom St George had snatched from the dragon's jaws.

It has been said (and the parallel is a good one) that the picture of St George tilting at the dragon with his lance recalls a heraldic emblem, so strongly does the dark image of the armed knight stand out against the distant sky. But Carpaccio certainly aimed at achieving more than this. In fact we may feel sure that he was intent on making the most of an exciting story, for his brush seems to linger over the macabre details of the dragon's half-devoured victims, wretchedly strewn over the hot sands where the only other sign of life are snakes, lizards and toads. And it lingers too over every tone and curve of the dragon's huge body, and minutely delineates the balconies, towers and minarets of the intricate hillside town in the distance.

There also reappears (as in the *Legend of St Ursula*) the old method of composing landscapes out of "prefabricated" parts: memories of travels abroad and reminiscences of prints and pictures he had seen. Visible to the left of the dragon, for example, is the Gate of Cairo, with its twin towers and drawbridge, painted with such painstaking accuracy that again it is impossible not to feel that the artist must have seen it with his

ST GEORGE AND THE DRAGON, C. 1507. (4 FT. 7 IN. × 11 FT. 9½ IN.)
SCUOLA DEGLI SCHIAVONI, VENICE.

own eyes. A wealth of details bring the figure of St George
vividly to life, from his shining armor to the spectacular trap-
pings of his horse. The color scheme has a richness and density
of tone that bring to mind Cosimo Tura's San Giorgio altarpiece from Ferrara. Yet, for all the care lavished on detail, the
general effect of the picture is harmonious and unified, with a
carefully adjusted balance of contrasting masses whose solemn
harmony is more grandiose than in any of the previous scenes
because the perspective vista is built up on broader, freer lines.

The fact is that, instead of building on a rigorous system
of coulisses which recede toward the vanishing point, Carpaccio
seems to have banked for his effects on a looser, more dynamic
scheme of composition, playing off masses against each other
in four triangular areas of the picture bounded by diagonals:
the town and dragon, the patch of ground strewn with corpses,
the knight and the princess behind him, the distant landscape
and sky. Several years had elapsed since the *Death of St Jerome*,
and *St George and the Dragon* is datable about 1507 (or shortly

THE TRIUMPH OF ST GEORGE, C. 1507. (4 FT. 8¼ IN.×11 FT. 7 IN.)
SCUOLA DEGLI SCHIAVONI, VENICE.

before), in which year the Schiavoni decorations were completed. (The landscape background stands very close to that of the Gulbenkian *Virgin and Two Donors adoring the Child*, dated 1507.) Carpaccio's style has gained much in the way of richness and variety by his deeper awareness of the constructive value of color. Without repudiating the past, this was the path he pursued in the future, with increasing freedom of expression.

Even in the adroit geometry of the *Triumph of St George*, with its carefully echeloned figure group tapering toward a vanishing point directly behind the saint's head, there is room for arresting plays of color boldly and freely applied. Witness the pair of horses on the right, the dark one pawing at the ground, head down, the white one rearing up proudly, to the tinkle of the glittering bells on its harness; or the court dignitaries in bright costumes of fine damask whose golden threads flash in the sunlight; or the procession of bandsmen drumming and piping away, while the king of Selene rides forward with his queen, holding his miraculously delivered daughter by the hand.

ST GEORGE AND THE DRAGON (DETAIL), C. 1507.
SCUOLA DEGLI SCHIAVONI, VENICE.

The broad square is like an unmarked chessboard on which
Carpaccio has skillfully maneuvered his "pieces" into position:
king and queen, knights, bishops and castles. Moving vividly
to its conclusion, the game is held in suspended animation for
a moment by the master hand of the artist; only the colors

ST GEORGE AND THE DRAGON (DETAIL), C. 1507.
SCUOLA DEGLI SCHIAVONI, VENICE.

continue to glisten and light to sparkle. So great is the evocative power of the scene, with bright figures caught in the slanting rays of the unseen sun, that we almost overlook the presence (as usual) of "prefabricated" elements: the figures of a court dignitary and two serving women borrowed from woodcuts

THE TRIUMPH OF ST GEORGE (DETAIL), C. 1507.
SCUOLA DEGLI SCHIAVONI, VENICE.

by Reeuwich (a preparatory drawing of this detail, in the Mather Collection, Washington Crossing, Pa., has led Tietze and Tietze-Conrat to conclude that similar drawings by Gentile Bellini are the common source from which both Reeuwich and Carpaccio drew). This picture, moreover, is crammed with "souvenirs" of Jerusalem: from left to right, the tower and the church of the Holy Sepulchre, the tower of the Mosque of Rama, and the Temple of Solomon.

This is not the place for an exhaustive discussion of these and other "recollections" of a voyage to the Levant (though in the *Triumph of St George*, even more so than in previous works, they have an accent of reality that almost compels the belief that at some time or other Carpaccio must have made such a voyage). It need only be noted here that, whenever he dwells on a quaint or colorful detail, Carpaccio's keen powers of observation seem to flag and, pursuing his fancy, he loses interest for a moment in the plausibility of his narrative.

Hence the inimitable charm of that narrative. Carpaccio was the liveliest illustrator of his time. The story he tells is always a personal reconstruction, fancifully embroidered on, and always tending to unfold on an abstract plane of pure enchantment. Such is the world in which his figures move, and such is the shared imaginative perspective in which they must be seen. Hence the increasing isolation in which Carpaccio came to stand in his own day and age. For these were the years—the first decade of the 16th century—in which Giorgione was painting the *Three Philosophers* and the *Tempest*, blending and shading colors in an atmosphere of expansive sensuality that seemed to pluck the mystery from the heart of nature. This was the atmosphere of the High Renaissance, and the 16th-century Venetian painters breathed it joyfully, moving through nature like Titans, exulting in emotions, tonalities, and visionary conceptions which they felt to emanate from nature herself. For them a landscape,

THE BAPTISM OF THE KING, 1507? (4 FT. 8¼ IN.×9 FT.)
SCUOLA DEGLI SCHIAVONI, VENICE.

whether trees or mountains, seas or city, was always intensely
real, intensely felt, and thereby recast in terms of the artist's
own experience. But such was not the case with Carpaccio;
he was a man of the "old school," an incurable Primitive who
saw the world in terms of preconceived ideas expressed in
accordance with set rules. The result is a self-sufficient world
whose conventions the mind is willing enough to accept, but
which fails to awaken any echo in the more vital consciousness
of our own experience.

Here we touch on the immediate reasons for the crisis in
Carpaccio's career which, almost as soon as he had finished
the Schiavoni decorations, stunted his growth as a painter at
a time when his ripening powers seemed to promise a brilliant
future. Probably without realizing what had happened, he found
himself unexpectedly compromised; Giorgione's innovations left

THE MIRACLE OF ST TRYPHONIUS, C. 1507. (4 FT. 8 ¼ IN. × 9 FT. 4 ½ IN.)
SCUOLA DEGLI SCHIAVONI, VENICE.

him at a disadvantage which he never overcame. He was still master of his "craft," but only in the old sense of the word, and now that the ground of art had shifted so radically his own style and methods were dismissed by his contemporaries as hopelessly old-fashioned. He struggled for a time against the current, then sank into oblivion.

Thus, by his inability to cope with these revolutionary developments, Carpaccio never acceded to the new way of seeing initiated by the two great artists of the Venetian Renaissance: Giovanni Bellini and Giorgione. It is important to bear in mind these circumstances, since they explain a decline and fall which might otherwise seem premature and incomprehensible. At less than fifty years of age, when his career should have been at its height and his position secure, he was forced to surrender the field to others.

THE BAPTISM OF THE KING (DETAIL), 1507? SCUOLA DEGLI SCHIAVONI, VENICE.

Still he was not without employment. First he brought the St George series to a conclusion with the *Baptism of the King*, a work entirely composed of "prefabricated" elements: the band playing on the platform, the horsemen ambling across the open square, the lady-in-waiting with the cylindrical head-piece, the elegantly designed (but by now familiar) flight of steps in the foreground. For the first time the background architecture smacks strongly of the stage-set. Buildings are projected in rough perspective toward the vanishing point, which lies to the right of the rider in a white turban. The composition fails to carry conviction; it is airless, prosaic, and shows signs of weariness and impoverished invention.

However, there are still some charming details: the Turkey carpet on the platform, the huge red and white turbans of the court dignitaries, the green and ivory striped cape of the serving woman. The vibration of their colors is even deeper and more resonant than in earlier works, absorbing light instead of reflecting it, enriching colors with a thousand tonal shadings. Carpaccio had always followed a characteristic path of his own, and his work lies outside the main line of evolution that led from Bellini to Giorgione. Although he sometimes makes unexpected contact with them, it was an exchange by which Carpaccio, by the very nature of things, could never stand to benefit, an exchange which for him inevitably signified a concession to their melodious sensuality; and this was a quality incompatible with his own gifts.

His hesitation and cross-purposes are only too evident in the last picture he painted at the Schiavoni: the *Miracle of St Tryphonius*, in which the saint exorcizes a devil from the daughter of the Emperor Gordian. Again we find the familiar architectural décor and echoes of the Venetian scene, but now there is an unmistakable sense of weariness; the happy dream of the Schiavoni had come to an end.

THE PRESENTATION IN THE TEMPLE (DETAIL), 1510.
GALLERIE DELL'ACCADEMIA, VENICE.

AFTER THE SCHIAVONI

WITH the completion of the Schiavoni decorations in 1507, the last chapter of Carpaccio's career begins: a fifteen-year period of irremediable maladjustment, as he carried on a losing struggle against time and the new spirit of the age.

He found himself adrift in an age of transition, and his efforts to contend with a new art world in the making are one of the most touching episodes in the story of early 16th-century Venetian painting. The same problems had to be faced by his fellow artists. Some, like Mantegna (d. 1506) and Giovanni Bellini (now over eighty), were flexible enough to keep abreast of new developments—or had originality enough to initiate them. Others, like Gentile Bellini (d. 1507) and Cima da Conegliano (d. 1518), went on living in an ivory tower, practising an archaic style which evolved very little. But all these men (except Mantegna of course) were Venetian to the core, and whether they changed with the times or stood still they drew their strength from a centuries-old tradition, a common artistic background.

Carpaccio had a different background and a different outlook. In early youth he pursued his wayward bent, serenely building castles in the air, for such was his inimitable *Legend of St Ursula*. He was a dreamer who woke up too late to the cultural movement that had been gathering momentum all around him. He engrossed himself in his visions at the Schiavoni, weaving into them a little of the color of the new Venetian school, but he remained at heart a solitary Primitive. He was like a small diamond of the first water in a brightly jewelled setting that dims its luster. He might have gone on as usual in his own vein, but he seems to have lost heart. He tried to come to terms with the new movement, making concessions of his own and borrowing whatever might serve his turn.

His last fifteen years of activity tell the story of this endeavor, an unfortunate one in every way. Carpaccio gained nothing by renouncing the kaleidoscopic fascinations of his old style, the shadow-theater of his perspective vistas, the indefinable charm of a narrative pitched midway between anecdote and symbol, between reality and formal abstraction.

With Giovanni Bellini and Cima da Conegliano perfecting the new theme of the Madonna in a landscape setting, with Lorenzo Lotto painting his first mythological "romances" and Giorgione at work on his Castelfranco altarpiece, Carpaccio chose to follow suit. He embarked on a stubborn attempt to make his mark in a field unfamiliar to him and, perhaps in spite of his better judgment, committed his story-telling powers to an objective description of nature—nature stripped of symbolism and rendered for her physical beauties alone.

It is hard to say what prompted him to imitate Bellini's Giovanelli *Madonna* and Sebastiano del Piombo's Giorgionesque *Virgin and Child* at Oxford so explicitly as he did in the small panel in Washington known as *A Saint Reading*, which almost certainly represents the Virgin with (before the panel was cut down) the Child beside her on the parapet; indications of the original theme are still visible beneath the retouchings. There is another *Virgin and Child* (Washington), also two figures representing *Temperance* and *Prudence* (Kress Collection, High Museum of Art, Atlanta, Ga.); all date from the first decade of the 16th century, and all are uneasily patterned on models by Cima and Giorgione which Carpaccio had only half assimilated.

This was the pitfall that beset him. Enamored before of linear perspective, he ventured now, candidly unmindful of his boldness, into the baggage-train of painters who had in the fullness of time absorbed a naturalistic culture and forged for themselves a musical style of tonal painting, the mature expression of the true Venetian genius. These painters were ripe for

A SAINT READING, C. 1504. (30¾ × 20″)
NATIONAL GALLERY OF ART, WASHINGTON, D.C. SAMUEL H. KRESS COLLECTION.

THE VIRGIN AND TWO DONORS ADORING THE CHILD, 1507. (35 $^5/_{16}$ × 53 $^5/_{16}$")
NATIONAL GALLERY OF ART, WASHINGTON, D.C.
C.S. GULBENKIAN COLLECTION (LOAN).

the transition to the cosmic vision of the High Renaissance,
Carpaccio was not. He had remained a Primitive at heart and
his attempts to practise the new art were a signal failure.

The box-like parapet of *A Saint Reading*, which only serves
to isolate and truncate the figure, was a flagrant anachronism in
the Venice of 1500-1510. Who else but Carpaccio would have
placed the figures of *Temperance* and *Prudence* in such precarious
equilibrium on the edge of the terrace? They look like manikins

about to topple over into the landscape whose every tree and blade of grass is delineated with naïve precision. What a difference from the contemporary work of Giorgione, whose "Judith" stands at the edge of the shadow cast by a large elm in counter-balance to the broad seascape background.

But Carpaccio's most unfortunate piece of work at this period is undoubtedly his cycle of decorations at the Scuola degli Albanesi, a small guild-hall built in 1489 near the church of San Maurizio. Scuola records for the year 1500 mention

THE FLIGHT INTO EGYPT, C. 1507. (28 ¼ × 43 ⅞")
NATIONAL GALLERY OF ART, WASHINGTON, D.C. MELLON COLLECTION
(WHERE IT IS ASCRIBED TO GIOVANNI BELLINI).

paintings in the Sala dell'Albergo. These were probably the first of Carpaccio's six small canvases illustrating the life of the Virgin. Dispersed after the fall of the Venetian Republic in 1797, they are now divided between the Accademia Carrara in Bergamo *(Birth of the Virgin)*, the Brera in Milan *(Presentation and Marriage)*, the Ca' d'Oro *(Annunciation and Death)* and Museo Correr in Venice *(Visitation)*. The *Annunciation* bears the date 1504, which probably represents the halfway point in the painting of the series.

There is little to be said for these works. None of them rises above a very pedestrian level. Anyone who compares these platitudes with the enchantments of the St Ursula series is forced to conclude that they must to some extent be the work of studio assistants. Yet, whatever the extent of that collaboration, their imagery is so pale a shadow of the imaginative beauties of the best work at the Scuola di Sant'Orsola and the Schiavoni that they can only be regarded as striking proof of Carpaccio's exhausted inventive powers. He had ceased to believe in his own poetry and was incapable of renewing himself.

The *Virgin and Two Donors adoring the Child* (Gulbenkian Collection, National Gallery, Washington) is signed and dated 1507. This picture is stylistically akin to the much-discussed *Flight into Egypt* which many critics, dating it to about 1480, still ascribe to Giovanni Bellini in view of Carpaccio's youthfulness at that time. For my part, I prefer to assign it to Carpaccio and date it to the first decade of the 16th century, when the artist was casting a more interested (though inveterately "primitive") eye at the works of Bellini and Cima da Conegliano; this interpretation of the facts seems altogether more plausible and gives the *Flight into Egypt* a fitting place in the pattern of Carpaccio's development.

Both the *Flight* and the *Virgin and Two Donors adoring the Child* are remarkable for their poetic qualities. The latter recalls the

Adoration by Gentile Bellini in the National Gallery, London (which Carpaccio copied in part in a drawing at the Uffizi), but it also reverts to the composition of the Schiavoni *Death of St Jerome*. The Child is the pivot on which the perspective hinges, while behind extends a diaphanous landscape. The strength of the picture lies in the full-bodied figures of Mary and Joseph and those of the two donors, both portrayed in sumptuous anachronistic costumes and both full of the breath of life.

Carpaccio has not yet succeeded, however, in integrating the figures into their setting. Again he has isolated them on a kind of forestage, a narrow, well-lit platform which stands distinctly apart from the landscape, to which it gives no apparent access. "Nature," then, is allowed to approach the stage of action but not to encroach on it, and the background stretches away in perspective till it is lost in a tenuous, light-filled haze. The well-marked foreground, on the other hand, projects sharply toward us, its "spearhead" being the Child himself with his light-hued skin.

This is the same composition as in the *Death of St Jerome*. There, however, a rigorous application of perspective elucidated every detail of the background and laid bare the well-articulated "masonry" of cube upon cube, organizing a spatial depth whose poetic undertones might be described as suspended lyricism. Here, in the *Virgin and Two Donors*, an interplay of tonal passages (in the color shadings of the distant background, in the chromatic density of the drapery) tends to arrest the imaginative sweep of the picture and denotes an increasing vagueness of purpose.

The figures in the *Flight into Egypt* also stand in isolation on a kind of forestage, very similar to that in the *Virgin and Two Donors*: a narrow path, bordered with stones, beside a field. The broad arc of a placid river leads the eye into a restful, far-flung landscape. There is an archaic note to the scene, and strains of an almost monodic music seem to accompany the easy gait of the donkey. We may not yet hear the lute music of Giorgione, but we catch a few echoes of the rustic pipes of Cima da Conegliano, whose influence is obvious in the ample, lucidly delineated figure of Mary, as it is in the vaporous landscape where a small boat (a Venetian "caorlina" and not the first one Carpaccio has shown us) glides downstream past a cluster of houses.

Finally, to convince ourselves that here we have Carpaccio's post-1500 style, it is enough to compare this painting with the Washington *Virgin and Child* and the Gulbenkian *Virgin*, remembering that the *Flight into Egypt* is separated stylistically from the *Legend of St Ursula* by a distance in time at least equal to the distance separating Giorgione from Giovanni Bellini's *Allegory* in the Uffizi (datable to about 1490)—and this *Allegory* has nothing in common with the *Flight into Egypt*.

The lush vegetation of the *Flight into Egypt* recurs, almost in the leading role, in the *Warrior* (Castle Rohoncz Museum, Lugano), throwing an aura of poetry over the scene. Carpaccio's powers as a narrator were far from exhausted if he could still give us so vivid an illustration of the stock medieval theme of the handsome knight drawing his sword before a castle, as the gates open and a mounted lancer issues forth followed by a mastiff. Projecting from the castle wall above the lancer is the sign of a galloping horse, as if the place were an inn or hostelry; perhaps it is a relay station, defended by walls and towers, on some mysterious frontier. There is indeed an element of mystery here, and a touch of the North, a touch of Dürer, in the figure of the knight—almost certainly a portrait, now impossible to identify. Perhaps there is significance too in the swooping falcon about to close on its prey, while frightened sparrows wheel in the sky. And those strange gardens alive with animals: a dog, rabbits, a heron, a deer, a peacock, and a ferret half hidden among the roses and wild lilies.

WARRIOR, C. 1507. (85 × 59½")
CASTLE ROHONCZ MUSEUM, LUGANO, SWITZERLAND.

Now this sudden predilection for motifs reminiscent of the great German master was certainly symptomatic; it was not an accidental shift of interest. First of all Dürer's art, with its unfailing sharpness of definition, its lucid descriptive and narrative power, could not but be congenial to Carpaccio. Both men—each in his own way, and indeed on very different levels—took the expressionistic approach to art. Further, the perfectly molded form and impeccable draftsmanship of Dürer, who was well known at Venice where he stayed briefly in about 1495 and at greater length in 1506-1507, might have struck Carpaccio as an ideal antidote to everything that was elusive and melting in the melodious wistfulness of Bellini and Giorgione. Dürer's best qualities might have struck Carpaccio, in his perplexity, as the requisites of a classical style capable of facilitating his own admittance into the magic circle of the new painting.

Undoubtedly there is a "neo-classical" veneer perceptible in the work of Carpaccio's last phase, from about 1500 on. Was this the only way out of the impasse into which he was led by his more or less deliberate (in any case reiterated) efforts to vie with Bellini and Giorgione? Perhaps Carpaccio himself felt that it was the only way, and thus in turn took up a position which was not a new one in Venice, for the architect Tullio Lombardo, in these very years, found himself in a similar predicament when he attempted to recast the naturalism of his early style in terms of classical modeling.

The foregoing explains why, in this period, Carpaccio also followed the example of Cima da Conegliano, at once the most classical and the most archaic of Venetian painters. Reminiscences of Cima occur notably in the Berlin *Virgin and Child with Two Saints* (now destroyed) and in *St Thomas enthroned between Two Saints* at Stuttgart (1507). The latter is an altar painting, commissioned by one Tomaso Licinio, from the church of San Pietro Martire at Murano, and in it Carpaccio obviously aims at fully plastic form almost crystalline in its burnished clarity, thus reverting to his early predilection for Antonello da Messina. In the *Death of the Virgin* of 1508 (Ferrara Museum, formerly in the church of Santa Maria in Vado) a glowing limpidity of light effect is achieved and exploited to the full in the amazing *trompe-l'œil* of the immediate foreground, which seems to stand out, independent of the rest, like one of the large terracotta "Lamentations" which the sculptor Guido Mazzoni was just then producing for the churches of Ferrara and Modena.

The style of these paintings is characterized by the luster of smoothly polished forms. Such too is the style of the large altar painting of *St Ursula in Glory* which, though it bears the date 1491, was almost certainly painted (or totally repainted) very much later than the *Legend of St Ursula*. It is a matter of record that in 1504 the Scuola di Sant'Orsola was reorganized internally and the position of the altar was changed. Perhaps Carpaccio took the opportunity of repainting an early work with which he was now dissatisfied; this would explain the otherwise unacceptable date of 1491. For the style coincides unmistakably with that of the works we have just been discussing; it is a style devoid of poetic fancies and confined (as in the Stuttgart and Ferrara panels) to the quest of a purely technical perfection in marked contrast to the freshness and lyricism of the *Legend of St Ursula.*

This change of style can hardly be described as a happy one. The results were inevitably couched in the stilted language of "neo-classicism"; his unfortunate aim was that illusion of the eclectic which goes by the name of *le beau idéal*, and which has always proved fatal to a genuinely poetic inspiration. This approach to painting, with its set program and eclectic aspirations, signalizes a whole episode in the silent struggle carried on, in vain, against the "revolutionary" tendencies of Venetian painting. Carpaccio seemed to turn to classicizing forms as a last, hastily erected bastion against the invading tonalism of his great Venetian contemporaries.

In spite of all his efforts to stifle them, the charming remnants of Carpaccio's youthful poetic style reappear in a masterpiece which stands out as one of the final landmarks of his career: the *Presentation in the Temple* (Venice Academy), a large altar picture painted in 1510.

This *Presentation* originally stood in the Venetian church of San Giobbe, together with a large *Sacra Conversazione* by Giovanni Bellini, painted in the last years of the 15th century. The latter is a melodious complex of warm, vibrant tones in which the leading figures loom up like the heroes of a perfected, superhuman world. No suggestion or even possibility of narrative or anecdote had any place in this majestic perfection, over-solemn perhaps but a masterpiece, if only by virtue of the flawless coherence of its forms. Again in 1505, this time in the church of San Zaccaria, Bellini painted a large altarpiece, representing the Virgin and saints in the niche-like recess of a temple. Here the velvet of the colors is spread over the picture surface with the density of a fully modulated crescendo, expressing the classical, monumental certitude of a world whose center is the artist himself, adding his note to that music whose strains had resounded of old in the golden vaults of St Mark's.

When Carpaccio painted his *Presentation in the Temple*, he no doubt regarded it as a last opportunity of pitting himself against Bellini and the new trend of Venetian painting. In front of the spacious niche containing the altar, the Virgin and Child and two serving women are met by Simeon and two deacons. Below, in a kind of orchestra pit, are three angel musicians playing a cromorne, a lute and a *lira da braccio* respectively. A glancing light comes in from the right; above, it gleams on a beautifully contrived chandelier of bronze and glass; below, it gleams on the slanted surfaces of the steps, sharply defining the chiaroscuro patterns on the smooth marble; it lengthens shadows into plummets that seem to probe the depths of the picture. Filtering into the interstices of the cornice that runs around the niche, light brings out every detail of the molding; it is focused on certain edges of the steps with an acuity that seems to make them razor-sharp. The two hexagonal prisms under the central angel and the rectangular ones to either side jut out from the "stage" like perfectly chiseled blocks of marble. The projection of the perspective is so well defined and the plastic value of forms is brought out so clearly as to suggest the precision of an architect's blueprint.

And all this is the creation of light as it impinges on an endless pattern of lines. It might be compared to the flow of a closely reasoned exposition of some exact science, whose logic is as precise and abstract as a mathematical equation. But what is the part played by color in this intricate piece of architecture? As it happens, color plays an important part, blended as it is in extremely thin layers of ductile pigment spread lightly and evenly over the plastic structure to produce a truly "luministic" effect which is virtually unique in Venetian painting. We should have to look to the School of Brescia, to such painters as Moretto and Savoldo, for a parallel. But they came on the scene somewhat later, and credit must go to Carpaccio for achieving such effects as early as 1510.

It is my personal conviction that the *Presentation* is a "polemical" picture, for it is quite unlike anything else in Carpaccio's output in this last phase. Resorting to a cold, carefully controlled luminism, and reducing the thickness of his paints to a light glaze, Carpaccio seemed to be adopting the best technical defense his medium could offer against the enticements of Giorgione's style. At least once, however, he consented to compete with Giorgione on the latter's own ground: in the picture usually known as *Two Courtesans* (Museo Correr, Venice).

"Color with light and shade" was Ruskin's summing up of this famous painting, which he described as "the best picture in the world." First of all, color. In the soft light focused on the figures two worlds seem to be confronted: that, placid yet sensual, of the two ladies (the coat of arms on the Majolica vase is that of the patrician Torella family) and the lively, frolicsome world of the pets keeping them company on the terrace. (Beyond this nothing more can be said, the panel having been cut down on two sides, below and to the left.)

Like a slow distillation, colors pass from modulation to modulation, golden yellow in the dress of one lady, dark green and red in that of her companion. Colors are bright and lively, lavishly applied and steeped in light, almost as if color for its own sake were the artist's aim. Thus for once in a way he relegates line (though it is line that determines the color scheme) to a humble position. Perspective too is of strictly secondary importance and figures are projected forward so as to emphasize the melodious reds and greens of garments, and also the white of their puffed sleeves. The very shadows glow with reflected colors. All these highly colored objects are harmoniously interdependent, yet each is fully alive, activated by its own lifeforce. Each has a warm tactile appeal; the fingers itch to touch and feel them.

Carpaccio's inspiration may have come from Giorgione, or from some Woman with a Mirror or some alluring Flora already imagined by Palma or Titian—but not necessarily. He might easily have been moved by the sight of a proud Venetian lady, in all her finery, enjoying the cool of the evening on her balcony, or preening herself in front of her mirror. Very possibly

TWO COURTESANS, C. 1510. (64½ × 37″) MUSEO CORRER, VENICE. ▶

Carpaccio was the first to imagine such a scene, even though the younger men, confidently destined for greater things, were soon to overshadow him completely.

A further episode in his struggle to keep pace with Giorgione is brought to light by a set of works in which, more openly than ever before, we see Carpaccio trying his hand at the characteristic figure grouping of the Giorgionesque "idyll." The curious thing is that Carpaccio makes his challenge with forms borrowed from Cima da Conegliano. Take, for example, the polyptych preserved in the small church of Grumello di Zogno. The figure of St Anthony Abbot is set into the landscape with so easy a mastery of naturalistic depth as to suggest that Carpaccio had at last acquired the knack of these effects. But such was not really the case. His handling of color has not evolved accordingly; minutely accurate in every detail, the charm of his color scheme lies wholly in its ornamental, not in its musical or atmospheric qualities, which are non-existent. Carpaccio, as usual, produces an *anecdote*, naïvely illustrated, not an *experience* imaginatively interpreted.

To the same group of narrative works belong two closely related paintings: the *Virgin and Child with Four Saints* (Caen) and the *Lamentation over the Dead Christ* (Berlin). In the Caen *Virgin and Child* the "orchestra" of the *Presentation in the Temple* reappears out of doors in the guise of two tiny angels, one jingling a tambourine, the other playing a harp. St Elizabeth and St Joseph seem to be listening to the music, while St Anne and St Joachim are absorbed in prayer. In the background, against a fanciful rock formation, various episodes in the life of St Jerome are illustrated.

The heart of the picture, however, beats in the depths of the landscape: an opulent walled city beside a river, beneath a towered castle on a crag. Truth or make-believe? This apparently mattered little to Carpaccio, provided he worked out the

VIRGIN AND CHILD WITH FOUR SAINTS, C. 1510. (37¾ × 49¼″)
MUSÉE DE CAEN.

rhythmic pattern of spatial composition which enabled him to
give breadth, light and life to objects and figures under a
southern sun, and to weld them into a unified whole.

The same stately rhythm and crystalline clarity characterize
the Berlin *Lamentation*, which perhaps is not so late a work as
generally supposed, but which in any case is closely akin to the

Caen *Virgin and Child*. It is strange to find in this very accomplished picture so much of that hallucinating luridness which we associate with the Ferrarese painter Ercole de' Roberti. As early as the 17th century the *Lamentation* was already in the Canonici Collection in Ferrara and it is tempting to surmise that it may actually have been painted in the city where, as we

LAMENTATION OVER THE DEAD CHRIST, C. 1510. (57⅛ × 72¾″)
STAATLICHE GEMÄLDESAMMLUNGEN, BERLIN.

have conjectured, Carpaccio may have received his early training. He is known to have kept in touch with Ferrara, where a certain number of his works were long preserved (e.g. the *Meditation on the Passion*, originally in the Canonici Collection, Ferrara, now in the Metropolitan Museum, New York).

The strong point of the Berlin *Lamentation* (as of so many of Carpaccio's paintings) is to be found in its details, from the amazing mortuary slab on which Christ's body is laid out, to the caves and queer rock formations. Its weak point is the separation of episodes and dispersal of action. Having gone too far in loosening up the framework of his perspective, Carpaccio lost his bearings and never quite succeeded in piecing together the multiple details of the picture complex. By dint of being "modern" in his approach, he ended up by treading the path that led him straight back to the microcosmic world of the Flemish Primitives—the very point from which his career had begun years before!

This is proof of the extent to which his style depended for its natural expression on the framework of linear perspective which served to organize his peculiar vision. Every time he ventured to dispense with that framework, his style suffered; over its gemlike brilliance crept a veil that blurred and dissociated the picture elements. His dogged attempts to keep abreast of new trends led him, willy-nilly, to the gradual repudiation of his delightful early style. The circle of his limitations had tightened around him; the years of decadence were at hand.

In 1510 the wool-merchants of Venice commissioned him to decorate their guild-hall, the Scuola di Santo Stefano, and in 1511 he finished the first canvas in the series: the *Communion of the Seven Deacons* (now in Berlin). This was followed in 1514 by *St Stephen disputing with the Doctors* (Brera) and, very probably, *St Stephen preaching* (Louvre). The concluding scene is the *Martyrdom of St Stephen* (Stuttgart). Discernible here and there in

ST STEPHEN DISPUTING WITH THE DOCTORS, 1514. (58×67¾")
PINACOTECA DI BRERA, MILAN.

each of the four paintings is the characteristic touch, weak and
toneless, of Francesco Bissolo, a follower of Giovanni Bellini,
who must have been engaged as Carpaccio's assistant.

To illustrate the legend of this preacher saint and proto-
martyr, Carpaccio relied once again on his mastery of linear
perspective. Hence, in *St Stephen disputing*, the colonnade

ST STEPHEN PREACHING, C. 1514. (59¾ × 76¾")
LOUVRE, PARIS.

receding smoothly into the picture; in *St Stephen preaching*, the beautifully foreshortened view of Jerusalem with the Holy Sepulchre atop the hill and the Mosque of Omar on the left. In the background of the former are spirited touches in his best narrative vein: turbaned Turks in small groups gossiping in the shade of tall cypresses. We meet again with something of the

VIRGIN AND CHILD WITH FOUR SAINTS (DETAIL), C. 1510.
MUSÉE DE CAEN.

ST STEPHEN DISPUTING WITH THE DOCTORS (DETAIL), 1514.
PINACOTECA DI BRERA, MILAN.

expressive power of the Schiavoni paintings, particularly in the tight focusing of all eyes on the figure of the young saint preaching, and in the glow of warm amber colors in the open space beyond the figure group; the tender green of those lawns brings to mind the tremulous glazes of *St Jerome in his Study*.

Carpaccio's last years were spent between various towns in the provinces of Venetia and Istria. The demand for his work had greatly diminished, and the commissions he received became smaller in scale and less remunerative. He had outlived his day and now found himself relegated to that second rank of artists whose work, disdained by the connoisseurs of Venice itself, was henceforth acceptable only to provincial tastes. Thus he was commissioned to do altar paintings at Capodistria (1516), Pirano and Pozzale di Cadore (1518), and Chioggia (1520), together with a few minor works in Venice, such as the *Martyrdom of the Ten Thousand on Mount Ararat* for the church of Sant'Antonio di Castello (1515), the polyptych for Santa Fosca (1514), and the tiny *St George and the Dragon* for San Giorgio Maggiore (1516). The last-named painting is a much enfeebled transposition, in the manner of Giorgione, of the more grandly conceived Schiavoni *St George*. Carpaccio's inexhaustible narrative vein found an outlet in the predella: four tiny scenes (by far the best part of the work) illustrating the martyrdom of St George.

But these painted decorations on the predella (i.e. the base) of an altarpiece were by this time so old-fashioned that we can almost imagine the smile of irony or condescension with which they must have been regarded by Titian, for example, who was just then working on the preliminary drawings for his great *Assumption of the Virgin* in the church of the Frari.

Whatever its charm or ingenuity, no picture of his could seem anything but anachronistic and "primitive" beside such work as this. Carpaccio had no alternative but a kind of enforced retirement which left him free to muse at leisure on past

THE LION OF ST MARK, 1516. (4 FT. 6¾ IN. × 12 FT.) DUCAL PALACE, VENICE.

triumphs. He might have strolled beside the lagoon and watched the stately galleons, home from the fancied voyages of Ursula and her companions. Perhaps, in the evening of life, he contemplated the Ducal Palace, the Campanile, the domes of St Mark's, and remembered with a sense of pride that no one had portrayed them better than he. Then, almost as a parting gesture, he painted the *Lion of St Mark* for the Palazzo dei Camerlenghi at the Rialto: the full expanse of the Venetian lagoon, from the Dogana da Mar to San Giorgio Maggiore to Piazza San Marco—his wayward brush brought them to life for the last time. It was a lesson of love, almost a heritage, which he transmitted to the Venetians of a later day who best understood him: Canaletto, Bellotto, Francesco Guardi. And they handed down the gist of his message to the great landscape painters of the Impressionist era.

Carpaccio died in such complete obscurity that the exact date of his death has never been ascertained. But he left his own memorial behind him and it will perpetuate his name as long as the human sensibility responds to the art of painting.

SELECTED BIBLIOGRAPHY

INDEX OF NAMES

CONTENTS

SELECTED BIBLIOGRAPHY

G. VASARI, *Delle vite de' più eccellenti pittori, scultori, ed architettori* (ed. Milanesi), vol. III, Florence 1878. — M. BOSCHINI, *Carta del navegar pitoresco*, Venice 1660. — C. RIDOLFI, *Le Meraviglie dell'Arte*, Venice 1668. — A. ZANETTI, *Della pittura veneziana*, Venice 1771. — L. LANZI, *Storia pittorica*, Bassano 1818. — J. RUSKIN, *St Mark's Rest*, Orpington (Kent) 1877-84. — B. BERENSON, *The Venetian Painters of the Renaissance*, London 1894. — J. RUSKIN, *Fors Clavigera*, London 1896-99. — S. COLVIN, *Über einige Zeichnungen des Carpaccio...*, in *Jahrbuch der P. K.*, 1897, 193. — G. LUDWIG and P. MOLMENTI, *Vittore Carpaccio*, Milan 1906. — V. GOLOUBEFF, *Due disegni del Carpaccio*, in *Rassegna d'Arte*, 1907, 140. — L. VENTURI, *Le Origini della pittura veneziana*, Venice 1907. — R. FRY, *A Genre Painter...*, in *The Quarterly Review*, April 1908. — J. CROWE and G. B. CAVALCASELLE, *A History of Painting in North Italy*, London 1912. — D. VON HADELN, *Carpaccio* in THIEME-BECKER, *Künstler-Lexikon*, Leipzig 1912 etc. — A. VENTURI, *Storia dell'arte italiana*, vol. VII, Milan 1915. — D. VON HADELN, *Venezianische Zeichnungen des Quattrocento*, Berlin 1925. — B. BERENSON, *Italian Painters of the Renaissance* and *Italian Pictures of the Renaissance*, 2 vols., Oxford 1932. — G. FIOCCO, *Vittore Carpaccio*, Rome 1932; 2nd edition 1942; French edition, Paris 1931. — G. FOGOLARI, *Pre' Sebastiano Bastiani, suo padre Lazzaro e il Carpaccio*, in *Rivista di Venezia*, 1932, 279. — R. LONGHI, *Per un catalogo delle opere di V. Carpaccio*, in *Vita Artistica*, 1932, 1. — G. FIOCCO, *Nuovi documenti intorno a V. Carpaccio*, in *Bollettino d'Arte*, Sept. 1932. — G. FIOCCO, *A proposito dei pittori L. Bastiani e V. Carpaccio*, in *Rivista di Venezia*, 1933, 31. — R. VAN MARLE, *The Development of the Italian Schools*, vol. VIII, The Hague 1936. — C. L. RAGGHIANTI, *Due Disegni del Carpaccio*, in *Critica d'Arte*, 1936, 277. — H. TIETZE and E. TIETZE-CONRAT, *The Drawings of the Venetian Painters in the 15th and 16th Centuries*, New York 1944. — R. LONGHI, *Viatico per cinque secoli di pittura veneziana*, Florence 1946. — R. LONGHI, *Calepino Veneziano*, in *Arte Veneta*, 1947, 188. — T. PIGNATTI, *Vittore Carpaccio*, Milan 1955. — M. MURARO, *Vittore Carpaccio alla Scuola degli Schiavoni*, Milan 1956. — T. PIGNATTI, *Proposte per la data di nascita di Vittore Carpaccio e per la identificazione della Scuola di S. Orsola*, in *Atti del XVIII° Congresso di Storia dell'Arte*, Venice 1956. — B. BERENSON, *Italian Pictures of the Renaissance, Venetian School*, 2 vols., revised and enlarged edition of the Berenson Lists, London 1957.

INDEX OF NAMES

Venice, Scuola degli Schiavoni (1502-1507) 8, 47, 55/81, 83, 88, 103, 106:
Vocation of St Matthew 56; *Prayer in the Garden* 56;
St Jerome in his Study 57/61, 64, 70, 106; *St Jerome and the Lion* 62, 64, 66, 67; *Death of St Jerome* 63, 65, 68, 69, 72, 89;
St George and the Dragon 71, 72, 74, 75, 106; *Triumph of St George* 71, 73, 76, 77; *Baptism of the King* 78, 80, 81;
Miracle of St Tryphonius 79, 81;

Venice, Scuola degli Albanesi (*Scenes from the Life of the Virgin*, ca. 1504) 8, 87:
Bergamo, Accademia Carrara: *Birth of the Virgin* 88;
Milan, Pinacoteca di Brera: *Presentation* and *Marriage of the Virgin* 88;
Venice, Ca' d'Oro: *Annunciation* and *Death of the Virgin* 88;
Venice, Museo Correr: *Visitation* 88;

Venice, Scuola di Santo Stefano 8, 101:
Berlin-Dahlem, Museum: *Communion of the Seven Deacons* 101;
Milan, Pinacoteca di Brera: *St Stephen disputing with the Doctors* 101, 102, 105;
Paris, Louvre: *St Stephen preaching* 101, 103;
Stuttgart, Gemäldegalerie: *Martyrdom of St Stephen* 101.

Other works:
Atlanta, High Museum of Art, Kress Collection: *Temperance* and *Prudence* 84, 86;
Berlin-Dahlem, Museum: *Lamentation over the Dead Christ* 17, 98/100; *Virgin and Child with Two Saints* (destroyed) 92;
Caen, Musée: *Virgin and Child with*

Four Saints (ca. 1510) 98, 99, 104;
Capodistria, Duomo: *Virgin and Child with Saints* (1516) 8, 106; *Altarpiece* (1523) 8;
Chioggia, San Domenico: *St Paul* (1520) 8, 106;
Ferrara, Pinacoteca: *Death of the Virgin* (from Santa Maria in Vado, 1508) 17, 93;
Florence, Contini Collection: *Christ with Four Disciples* (ca. 1490) 11/13;
Florence, Serristori Collection: *Pietà* 52;
Florence, Uffizi: fragment of a *Crucifixion* (ca. 1495) 51;
Frankfort, Städelsches Institut: *Virgin and Child with St John* 52;
Grumello di Zogno: *Polyptych* 98;
London, National Gallery: *Scenes at a Tournament* (ca. 1490, also ascribed to Domenico Morone) 3, 4, 17;
Lugano, Castle Rohoncz Museum: *Warrior* (ca. 1507) 90, 91;
New York, Metropolitan Museum: *Meditation on the Passion of Christ* (ca. 1500) 17, 52, 53, 101;
Pirano (Istria), San Francesco: *Virgin and Child with Saints* (1518) 8, 106;
Pozzale di Cadore, parish church: *Virgin and Child with Saints* (1518) 8, 106;
Stuttgart, Gemäldegalerie: *St Thomas enthroned between Two Saints* (from San Pietro Martire, Murano, 1507) 92, 93;
Treviso, San Francesco: *Meeting of Anne and Joachim* (1515, now in Venice, Accademia) 8;
Udine, Museo Civico: *Christ* (1496) 52;
Venice, Ducal Palace: painting for the Sala dei Pregadi (1501-1502,

CONTENTS

THIS VOLUME, THE TWENTY-FOURTH OF THE COLLECTION "THE TASTE OF OUR TIME", WAS PRODUCED BY THE TECHNICAL STAFF OF EDITIONS D'ART ALBERT SKIRA, FINISHED THE THIRTY-FIRST DAY OF OCTOBER NINETEEN HUNDRED AND FIFTY-EIGHT

TEXT AND ILLUSTRATIONS BY

COLOR STUDIOS
AT IMPRIMERIES REUNIES S.A., LAUSANNE

PLATES ENGRAVED BY
GUEZELLE ET RENOUARD, PARIS

PHOTOGRAPHS BY

Zoltán Wegner, London (page 3), Claudio Emmer, Milan (pages 12, 15, 21, 22, 23, 25, 27, 28, 29, 31, 32, 33, 35, 36, 39, 40, 41, 42, 43, 49, 51, 58, 60, 61, 62, 63, 66, 67, 69, 72, 73, 74, 75, 76, 78, 79, 80, 82, 97, 102, 105, 107, and plates on dustjacket), Henry B. Beville, Washington (pages 53, 85, 86, 87, 91), Louis Laniepce, Paris (pages 99, 103, 104), Walter Steinkopf, Berlin (page 100), and by the photographic services of the British Museum, London, and Alinari, Florence, for the drawings reproduced on pages 18 and 26.

PRINTED IN SWITZERLAND